ADVANCED DUI INVESTIGATION

ABOUT THE AUTHOR

Dan Haggin is a twenty-year veteran of the Salt Lake County Sheriff's Office. He retired as a Sergeant in 1998. During his tenure as a Deputy Sheriff, he worked in Patrol, Detective, Juvenile, Traffic and Training. His passion, during his career, has been traffic accident investigation/reconstruction, DUI detection and training. Dan held posts as Training Supervisor for the Salt Lake Community College Police Academy and as an instructor for the Utah Peace Officer and Standards Academy.

He completed his undergraduate work in Criminal Justice Management in 1996 and graduate school in 2003 obtaining a Doctorate in Education degree.

Dan is married to his bride of five years. They have combined their families, and now include nine children and five grandchildren.

ADVANCED DUI INVESTIGATION

A Training and Reference Manual

By

DANIEL J. HAGGIN, Ed.D.

CHARLES C THOMAS • PUBLISHER, LTD.
Springfield • Illinois • U.S.A.

Published and Distributed Throughout the World by

CHARLES C THOMAS • PUBLISHER, LTD.
2600 South First Street
Springfield, Illinois 62704

This book is protected by copyright. No part of
it may be reproduced in any manner without
written permission from the publisher.

©2005 by CHARLES C THOMAS • PUBLISHER, LTD.

ISBN 0-398-07570-0 (spiral)

Library of Congress Catalog Card Number: 2004063795

With **THOMAS BOOKS** *careful attention is given to all details of manufacturing and design. It is the Publisher's desire to present books that are satisfactory as to their physical qualities and artistic possibilities and appropriate for their particular use.* **THOMAS BOOKS** *will be true to those laws of quality that assure a good name and good will.*

Printed in the United States of America
R-3-CAMRDY

Library of Congress Cataloging-in-Publication Data

Haggin, Daniel J.
   Advanced DUI investigation : a training and reference manual / by Daniel J. Haggin.
      p. cm.
   Includes index.
   ISBN 0-398-07570-0 (spiral)
    1. Drunk driving--Investigation--United States--Handbooks, manuals, etc. 2. Drunk driving--United States. 3. Drugged driving--United States. 4. Roadside sobriety tests--United States. 5. Police training--United States. I. Title.

HV8079.D76H34 2005

2004063795

This manual is dedicated to all of the street cops of this nation; past, present and future. You are "worth it," and your work is "worth it."

PREFACE

Every police officer who has attended a basic police academy has received a modicum of training in the detection and arrest of impaired or intoxicated drivers. I have participated in this type of training, both as a student and as an instructor, however, the time allotted for DUI training was at best, adequate, but was never completely satisfactory. Inservice training in the art and science of DUI investigations has also fallen short of the mark. In short, I was never able to obtain the training necessary to elevate myself to a level of competency on a par with the other professionals within the criminal justice/court system. There were no real formalized courses available to fill the void in the post academy training regimes.

It took a concerted effort, over many years, to research and locate all of the data I wanted and needed. Nevertheless, I was able to compile what I believe is a valuable collection of training information on the subject of DUI investigations. This information was put together into a syllabus and used to train many hundreds of police officers over a ten-year period.

This training and reference manual is, therefore, a compilation of twenty years of past successes and failures investigating impaired or intoxicated driver offenses. Successes were mentally cataloged for future use and the failures were thoroughly analyzed for their probative value with negative information discarded and the positive retained. My experiences have ranged from literally hundreds of simple traffic stop DUI's to catastrophic auto-homicide reconstructions.

The failure, on the part of many courts in the nation, to fully accept Horizontal Gaze Nystagmus Field Sobriety Testing has been a significant frustration over the years. I have included, therefore, extensive research into the legitimacy of this valuable field sobriety test as both an observational and a scientific test of an impaired human central nervous system.

This training manual was developed with two objectives in mind:

> 1. To compile into one volume, the information needed by a police officer to qualify them as an "expert."

2. To increase the confidence level of those everyday working street cops who must make decisions about whether to arrest or not arrest on any given impaired or intoxicated driver situation.

Towards that end, this manual was created to serve both as a text for in classroom training and/or carried in the patrol car for easy and quick reference. It will not enable an officer to be an attorney or toxicologist, but it will provide the basis for the street cop to excel in this field of law enforcement and, indeed, prepare themselves as an expert in the detection and arrest of DUI drivers.

DAN HAGGIN

ACKNOWLEDGMENTS

I must first and foremost, thank my wife Vera for her profound love and friendship. It was her understanding and motivating encouragement that allowed this manual to be completed. Thanks to Courtney, my daughter and Joshua, my son for their unending help. Courtney kept her composure and grace while endlessly pestered about the "look" of the manual and requests to help type many, many pages. Josh kept my old computer running during the hundreds of hours spent pounding on the keys.

How does one thank a person who so unselfishly gave of her time and expertise just to help. I don't know . . . but thank you Laura. Laura Gudmundson edited this manual page by page, line by line. Her gift and friendship are truly treasured.

I must also thank the National Highway Traffic Safety Administration for their encouragement and assistance.

To Vicki Clough, thanks for lovingly guiding and coaching me through some very difficult times, for "getting in my face" when I needed it and for allowing me the opportunity to find out that I am worth it.

Thanks to all of the Law Enforcement instructors who taught me the value of continued learning even when I thought I knew everything.

CONTENTS

Page

Preface vii

Chapter

1. BEHAVING SYSTEMS
   Introduction 3
   Section One: Elements of the Human Behavioral System: Brain,
   Spinal Cord and Associated Structures 9

2. IMPAIRING DRUGS
   Section One: Pharmacology and Toxicology of Drugs 39
   Section Two: Drug Effects on the Central Nervous System 42
   Section Three: Ethyl Alcohol 50
   Section Four: Depressant and Stimulant Drugs . . . and Others 83

3. INVESTIGATIVE PROCESS
   Section One: Introduction 111
   Section Two: Driving Patterns 114
   Section Three: Traffic Stop and Physical Demeanor 123
   Section Four: Field Sobriety Testing 131
   Section Five: Evidence and Report Writing 182
   Section Six: Court Testimony 194
   Section Seven: Case Law 201

Index 219

ADVANCED DUI INVESTIGATION

CHAPTER ONE: BEHAVING SYSTEMS
Introduction

Motor vehicles are the most common form of transportation in the United States and the greatest cause of death in this country. Many factors contribute to motor vehicle crashes including highway and vehicle design, traffic density, and driver error due to inexperience and lack of skill. However, the single most significant predictor of traffic collision risk is the driver's mental and physical state – their sobriety.

THE HUMAN INTELLECT AND THE MIND

As is true of all animal life here on earth, human being are basically biological organisms. However, the complex abilities of learning, thinking, social organization and cultural traditions are specific expressions of what is known as, the *"human biological potential."* In fact, the human race is a privileged species. Our distinct differences lie in what members of the human race, in comparison to all other animal life, can accomplish. For example, we as human being are able to imagine, design, manufacture and operate complex machinery. We are able to reason through compound problem-solving techniques and determine resolutions.

Also, it is important to understand that the human experience is based on the environment in which we exist. In other words, the mental functions of a person sitting in a beautiful field of wild flowers are much different than those needed by the same person when operating a motor vehicle on a crowded roadway. Furthermore, **"man"** possesses susceptibilities and observable, measurable characteristics as a consequence of being human. Within the context of this manual, alcohol and drugs produce predictable and quantifiable behaviors, which are easily observed and recorded.

Physiologically, all animal life is constructed of cells, organized into tissues and chemicals, and ultimately, into organs, subsystems and finally, whole systems. This configuration provides vital function and structural integrity for each individual body type within the animal kingdom.

What then, makes the human race any different from other animal life? Homo Sapiens, in contrast to other life, possess an incredibly sophisticated and intricate arrangement of specialized cellular bodies, tissues and organs, known as, **"The Central Nervous System"** (CNS). Other attributes, which distinguish the human species from all others, are:

- The ability to walk utilizing only the lower limbs while in an upright position, the prehensile hand that can act as a tool;
- The ability to develop technology;
- The development of speech and language, thus allowing more adaptable forms of communication;
- The enlargement of the brain in relation to the size of the body;
- The development of social and cultural interactions;
- Longer periods of childhood and youth, permitting a considerable more time for the development of social and cultural interaction with other species members;

- The division of tasks within our society and the control over aggression;
- The ability for human beings to express themselves as individuals through the involvement of emotion, motivation and artistic and spiritual expression.

All these characteristics, directly or indirectly, are related to the development of the cerebral cortex of the brain. Thus, humans possess a uniqueness that depends entirely upon the Central Nervous System. The enormous human brain, especially the cerebral cortex, endows the human species with properties that do not exist (or exist only in a primitive form) among other animal species. It is by means of this huge and complex system that we possess high levels of synthetic analysis, and it is in the cortex that our worldview is analyzed, planned and programmed to carry out thoughts and actions.

The human species has the singular capacity of controlling the emotional brain by means of the rational brain. It is believed that this skill, coupled with the ability to create complex plans, allows for creative thought through intelligence. All restrictions and physical weaknesses are supplanted or are overcome, because the CNS is able to overwhelm these limitations and create anew.

Scientific knowledge, with regards to the definition of "Intellect," is limited and certainly varied, because there is no clear-cut and concise definition for the word or the concept. However, "intellect" is generally understood to be "our ability to utilize what we know, perceive and foresee in an effort to find adequate solutions to problems and to create." To many philosophers the mind and the intellect are one and the same. Others believe them to be separate components. Nevertheless, a common philosophical definition for both is: The power of perceptual thought; the aggregate of all conscious and unconscious thought processes and cognition. Intelligence then, is evident in many different forms, making it very difficult to define and forces significant debate among the scientific and philosophical communities alike.

The phenomenon of intellect is present only in the human species and is responsible for the ability to possess and utilize **creative thought, have memory, will power, complex emotional feelings** and further, possess the **ability to change** etc. Thus, man is able to **reason, analyze and synthesize** information, all of which are prerequisites to **"understanding,"** and essential to **sound decision-making**.

It is the sum total of all these human capabilities, susceptibilities and characteristics, which are specifically and uniquely human, that make up the mind. They are at least included in, are the natural expression of, or are closely related in some way to those functions, which also make up the human intellect. In other words, the mind is the person and the person is the mind. One cannot function without the other.

Humans then, are conscious beings who share a common experience of, a sense of self, and of conscious awareness. However, the quest to explain it all in an uncomplicated fashion escapes everyone and is one of the last remaining adventures of science and philosophy.

The "mind" and "intellect" have what can be best be termed as being a "nebulous human characteristic." There is no certain way of pin-pointing their location or structure. Nevertheless, it is a scientific fact that in order for all of the distinct sensory functions of the mind and intellect to perform properly, and in turn, for a human being to behave normally, every structure, system, subsystem, and every process, conscious or unconscious, must be coordinated. This is accomplished by the CNS, which is in effect the communicating, integrating and thought-processing structure, the computer if you will, of the human body.

This unique and vastly complicated system is connected to a vast array of ancillary structures, which in turn provide sensory input and a means for neural impulses to travel from one point in or on the body, to any other point in or on the body. The brain, and to a certain extent, the spinal cord, coordinate all of these complex subsystems, and allow the **"Human Intellect"** and **"Mind"** to exist.

A consideration of these endowments is a logical starting point in the journey toward understanding human behavior and in particular, behavior impaired by alcohol and/or drugs.

It is the development of these attributes, which form the foundation of driving competence. Any interference with this delicate arrangement, such as the introduction of alcohol and/or other exogenous drugs, is of grave concern for a DUI investigator.

Through careful observation, a well trained and experienced police officer, utilizing concise scientific tests, can recognize a driver's mental and physical condition, gauge it against the "norm" of a sober person, and ultimately, make a decision as to whether or not they are impaired with respect to the operation of a motor vehicle. To accomplish this task, an officer must understand how the Central Nervous System is organized, how its varied functions interact and further, how alcohol and/or drugs impair this delicate and marvelous systemic balance.

> **It is the strength of the Human Intellect, and the ability to use its potential that sets us apart from other animal life.**

SECTION ONE:
Elements of the Human Behavioral System: Brain, Spinal Cord and Associated Structures.

It is the brain (and its connected organs), which is responsible for the manifestations of impairment, observed by Law Enforcement DUI/DWI investigators.

THE BRAIN

When alcohol and drugs are consumed, a definitive pattern of action and reaction takes place within the Central Nervous System. It is not just a simple matter of taking a drink with the result being intoxication. In fact, thousands, if not millions, of neurons are affected, and a like number of chemical processes take place. In order to fully understand the nature and extent of impairment, a study of the CNS and how alcohol and drugs affect its homeostasis must be undertaken. This will assist Law Enforcement Officers in testifying in a court as experts by providing a much broader educational foundation.

The brain is by far the largest mass of nerve tissue within the human body. It weighs approximately 3 pounds and contains about 100 billion nerve cells (neurons). Obviously, the cells, which make up the brain, are highly specialized, but they function according to the laws governing all physiological structures. Their electro-chemical signals can be detected, recorded, interpreted, and identified, and their connections mapped. In short, the brain can be studied.

It is the receiver and analyzer of all sensory information. It accomplishes these tasks by processing information within the various structures of the entire Central Nervous System. Some of the processes occur in only one organ, while others must utilize the processing power of several organs and indeed, sometimes the entire system is involved. Remember that there are approximately 100 billion neurons in the human brain. Each neuron has about 10,000 connections with other neurons. The complexity is enormous, but incredibly, the brain functions perfectly under every environmental condition when it is alcohol and drug free.

From the first moment of conception, a human embryo begins to develop by cell division. In a very short period of time, a neural canal (precursor of the spinal cord) is formed, and then the brain begins its formation. All vertebrate brains develop from three swellings at the anterior, or top end, of the neural canal. From front to back these develop into the **Forebrain (Prosencephalon), Midbrain (Mesencephalon) and the Hindbrain (Rhombencephalon)**. (See Figure 1)

Forebrain (Proencephalon)

The Forebrain is made up of the following structures:

Cerebrum
Thalamus
Hypothalamus

Cerebrum

Commonly known as "gray matter," the *Cerebrum* makes up the bulk (70% of all the cranial neurons) of the human brain. It appears as a mass of gray and white colored tissue, characterized by an extensively folded and convoluted exterior surface known as the

Cerebral Cortex. This Cortex provides a surface area large enough for the *"human intellectual thought processes"* to take place. It is within this outer expanse of neural tissue that higher mental activity such as **Reasoning, Creative Thought, Judgment and Memory** take place.

Neurophysiologists believe that it is the cerebral cortex that differentiates humans from all other living beings. Indeed, if one were to compare the size of the homosapien cerebrum to that of other advanced animal life, it would be readily apparent that the human cerebrum, and hence the cerebral cortex, is larger by far than that of any other species.

The interior portion of the cerebrum is composed of white matter bound together by bundles of neural fibers known as **"Tracts."** These tracts transmit impulses to and from the cerebral cortex and the interior areas of the brain. **"Association Tracts,"** are short and extend only from one fold to another within a specific hemisphere. Others extend from one hemisphere to another and are known as **"Commissural Tracts." "Projection Tracts"** extend from specific parts of the cerebrum through the brain stem, into other parts of the brain or into the spinal cord. Tracts located outside of the brain and spinal cord structures are known simply as **"Nerves."**

The Cerebrum is divided into two halves, or hemispheres, by the *Longitudinal Cerebral Fissure.* Each hemisphere is further divided into lobes known as **Frontal, Parietal, Occipital** and **Temporal**. Because the body's peripheral nerves "cross over" in various places within the spinal cord, the left hemisphere of the cerebrum controls the right side of the body and vice versa.

Frontal Lobe

The Frontal Lobe mass controls the following human functions:
- Voluntary Movement
- Motor Planning
- Aspects of Language and Speech Production
- Aspects of Emotion and Social Behavior
- Decision Making
- Working Memory
- Verbal Fluency

Parietal Lobe

The Parietal Lobe mass controls the following human functions:
- Somatosenses – Touch, Kinesthesis, Balance
- Spatial Perception/Spatial Neglect
- Spatial Maps of the World and Body
- Aspects of Reading and Visual-Auditory Integration
- Aspects of Memory

Occipital Lobe

The Occipital Lobe mass controls the following functions:
- Vision
- Visual Perception

Temporal Lobe

The Temporal Lobe mass controls the following functions:
- Aspects of Personality and Emotion
- Audition
- Auditory Perception and Memory
- Aspects of Language Comprehension

Thalamus	The Thalamus is located at the highest portion of the structure known as the brain stem. It serves as a relay for nerve impulses to and from the cerebral cortex. Furthermore, it receives and coordinates stimuli for pain relief.
Hypothalamus	The Hypothalamus regulates body temperature, carbohydrates and metabolism, water balance, and, of most importance, the autonomic functions of internal organs.
Midbrain (Mesencephalon)	Contains the following: **Reticular Formation** **Substantia Nigra** **Ventral Tegmental Area**
Reticular Formation	The *RT* is constructed of bundles of nerve fibers that extend outward in all directions. It controls the inhibitory and excitatory (Sympathetic or Parasympathetic) functions and is thought to be an integrating center influencing the activities of other parts of the CNS.
Substantia Nigra	The Substantia Nigra helps mediate "smooth out" body movements.
Ventral Tegmental Area	The Ventral Tegmental Area is packed with dopamine releasing neurons that synapse deep within the Forebrain. The VTA is considered the pleasure center. Amphetamines and cocaine bind to the same receptors that they activate.

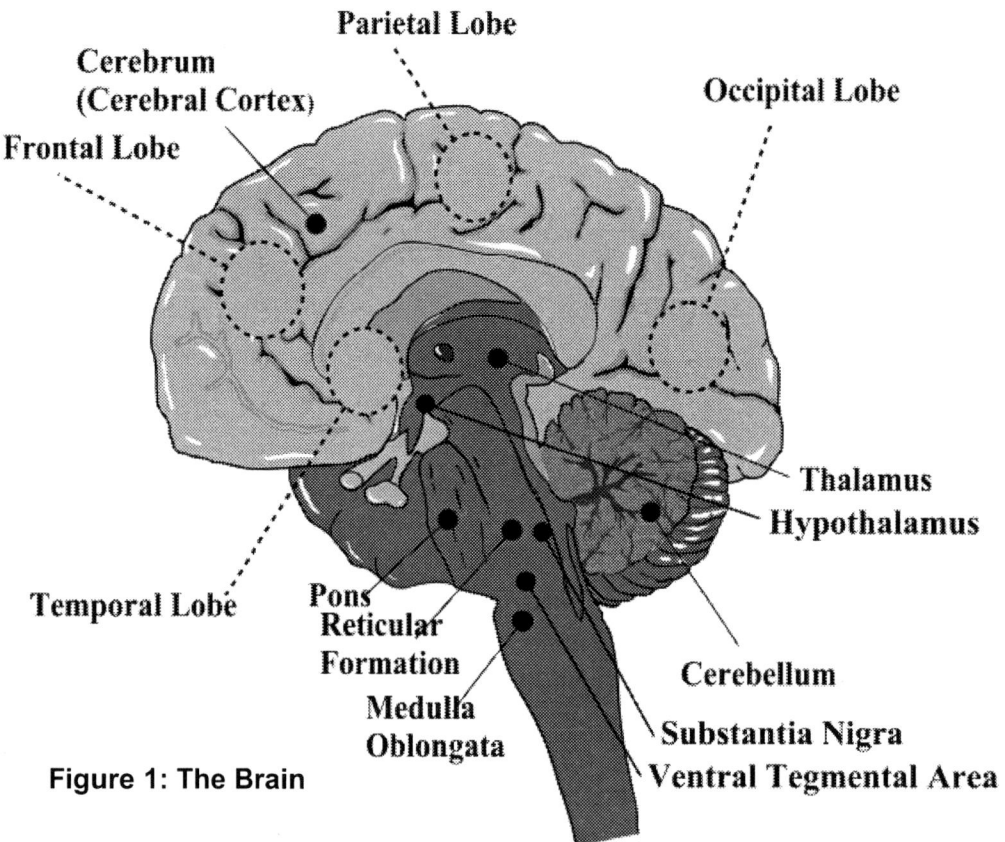

Figure 1: The Brain

Hindbrain (Rhombencephalon)	Contains the following structures: • **Cerebellum** • **Pons** • **Medulla Oblongata**
Cerebellum	The Cerebellum is an organ located between the brain stem and the hind part of the cerebrum. Its cortex, like that of the cerebrum, is composed of a sheath of nerve cells and fibers, and is wrinkled by parallel and curved furrows, or folia. It connects structures located

Pons within the brain stem, with the center of muscular activity within the cerebral cortex.

Neural impulses, received by the cerebellum, from skeletal muscles, joints, tendons, ligaments, semicircular canals and/or the motor area of the cerebrum, are sent to the muscular groups, necessary for maintaining body equilibrium. Generally speaking, these impulses do not enter the consciousness, yet the cerebellum "knows" what positions the different parts of the body occupy, and how to modify them to maintain balance. This is known as the science of ***kinesthetics***.

Impairment of the cerebellum produces dizziness, inability to coordinate the body muscles, resulting in jerky and inaccurate movements.

Pons The ***"bridge,"*** as the ***Pons*** is sometimes called, is an upward continuation of the spinal cord nerve tracts, and conducts impulses towards higher centers of the brain.

Medulla Oblongata The Medulla Oblongata is the part of the brain that directly attaches to the spinal cord. It is an enlarged extension of the cord and contains the connections for the cranial nerves, the muscles of the face, the senses of hearing and time, and controls the sensory and motor functions of the chest and abdominal organs.

Since it coordinates the impulses of the vital centers (heart, lungs, etc.), it is felt to be the most important organ of the entire brain. Quite simply, its proper functioning is crucial for sustaining life.

THE SPINAL CORD

The *Spinal Cord* is a longitudinally arranged organ, positioned on the posterior, or backside, of the human torso. It stretches from the brain stem, down the center of the back, to the beginning of the lumbar vertebrae, and contains nerve tracts, which transmit impulses to and from the brain. It contains organic components, which allow "*Reflex*" actions to take place.

Spinal Cord Functions

The spinal cord exercises three main functions:

1. It carries messages or nerve impulses from the body to the brain by means of the following:
   a) The white columns located on the posterior or backside of the cord carry impulses from sensory neurons originating in the muscles, tendons and joints, making possible the "*Kinesthetic Sense*." In other words, the sense of position and movement of the various parts of the body without actually looking to see where they are. If these tracts are injured or malfunction, a person's appendages cannot communicate to the brain or spinal cord, causing confusion of their spatial positioning. **This concept of human behavior is important to understand with respect to conducting Field Sobriety Tests.**

    b) The lateral or side columns carry impulses from heat, cold, pain and pressure source receptors of the skin and organs to the brain.

    c) Both the posterior and the lateral columns are the main "**ascending tracts**" of the spinal cord

2. It carries messages from the brain to the spinal nerves and finally to the muscles, glands and other organs of the body. These anterior or frontal columns of white matter are composed mainly of motor fibers. Disorder or disease of these columns produces paralysis to those body parts supplied by the level of the cord affected. They are known as the "*descending tracts.*"

3. Lastly, it carries out what are defined as *Reflex Acts* of the first level (see Page 28).

THE PERIPHERAL NERVOUS SYSTEMS
Somatic and Autonomic

In order for this entire system to operate properly, there must be a network in place that allows the transmission of nerve impulses to and from the brain and to permit corresponding physical and mental action and reaction to take place. This organization is known as the Peripheral Nervous System. It is divided basically into the Somatic Nervous system and the Autonomic Nervous System.

Somatic Nervous System

The somatic nervous system consists of peripheral nerve fibers that send sensory information to the Central Nervous System and motor nerve fibers that project to the skeletal muscles.

Autonomic Nervous System

The autonomic nervous system is divided into two functions that are of interest to a DUI investigator: the **sympathetic nervous system** and the **parasympathetic system.**

Sympathetic Nervous System

This system is generally located in the spinal cord areas of the body and is sometimes known as the Thoracic-Lumbar Outflow Region. It enables the body to be prepared for fear, flight or fight. Sympathetic responses include an increase in heart rate, blood pressure and cardiac output, a diversion of blood flow from the skin and splanchnic vessels to those supplying skeletal muscle, increased pupil size, bronchiolar dilation, and contraction of sphincters and metabolic changes.

Adrenaline and noradrenaline are both excitatory neurotransmitters which are synthesized and utilized by this system. They work very extensively with the neurotransmitter dopamine which can be both excitatory and inhibitory. (See section on Neurotransmission for additional information.)

Parasympathetic Nervous System

Again, this system is located within the spinal cord and brain stem areas of the CNS. It is centered in the high portion of the brain stem, and low in the sacral region of the spinal cord. It is therefore, sometimes known as the Cranio-Sacral Outflow. Acetylcholine, generally an excitatory chemical, is the predominate neurotransmitter synthesized and utilized by the parasympathetic system.

The parasympathetic system's function is the conservation and restoration of energy, as it causes a reduction in heart rate and blood pressure, and facilitates digestion and absorption of nutrient.

The cerebrospinal function is associated with the reception of stimuli from inside and outside the human body and the integration of these stimuli within the brain. In fact, it is the function that ties all of the various systems together and allows their proper operation. It processes such sensation as pain, temperature variation, touch, perception of weight and size, texture, configuration or shape of objects, awareness of the position of body parts, vibratory sense, taste, smell, sight and bearing, etc.

In general, there are three subsystems, functioning within the framework of the body, which enable all neural functions to take place.

- **Receptors**
- **Associators**
- **Effectors**

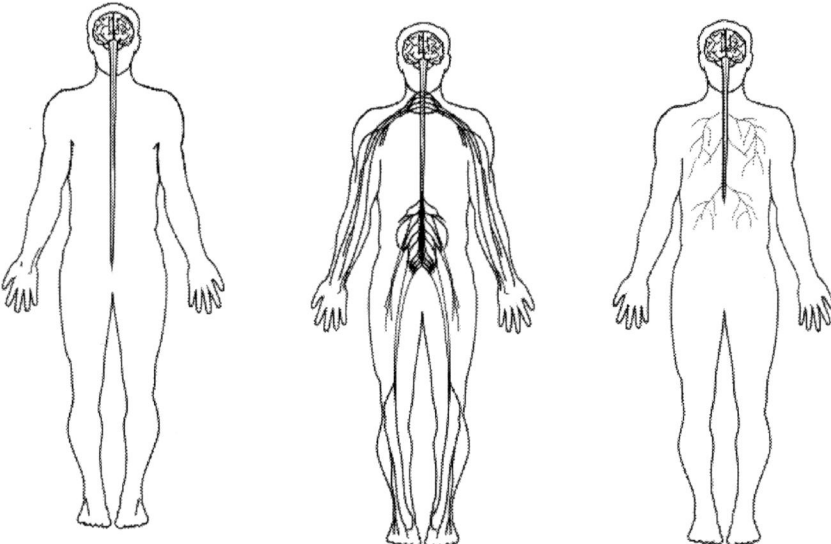

Figure 2: Central, Somatic and Autonomic Nervous Systems

Receptors

Receptors receive stimulation from the environment, which includes, in addition to stimuli from outside, those that initiate from within the body. They are, in fact, the various sense organs of the body. They vary in complexity, from the extremely intricate structures of the eyes and ears, to the relatively simple, free nerve endings of the skin.

The simplest forms of receptors are those whose dendrites are stimulated by external energy. They operate by converting some form of physical energy, such as light, sound, or movement of the skin into nerve impulses. In other words, information from the environment is transformed by the receptors from the physical and chemical forms received into the special electro-chemical code utilized by the CNS.

Sensations: In researching this section, it was found that the receptor is more commonly known by the term, ***sense organ.*** Funk and Wagnells, Standard Dictionary: International Edition defines sensation as "that aspect of consciousness resulting from the stimulation of a nerve process beginning at any point in or on the body and passing through the Central Nervous System."

In other words, sensations are physical or mental "human responses" to the environment. They are generated by stimulation of a receptor or receptors, and are interpreted by the Central Nervous System. If the senses and/or the CNS are impaired, the action/input processed by the entire system may be misinterpreted, misunderstood or not completed at all.

Characteristics of Receptors

Traditional Senses: The "traditional" five senses - hearing, vision, taste, smell and touch, are interrelated developments in the primate order in the ancestry of the human being. They are based on the major body structures that contain neural receptors, such as the eyes, ears, nose, tongue and skin. There is no question that if any of the traditional senses had been missing from the mixture during the evolution of man, we as humans could not have developed into what we are today.

Neural receptors differ greatly in both structure and levels of energy needed to cause stimulation; yet, all are alike in certain characteristics of operation.

1. The first characteristic is that **neural responses vary with the intensity of the stimulus**. For example, the response of the optic nerve is greater to bright lights than to dim lights. The sensory nerve increases in intensity in either of two ways:
    a) **Quicker response of the individual neurons.** Under intense stimulation, neurons will fire earlier in the relative refractory phase than under weaker stimulation.
    b) **Increase in the number of neurons that fire.** Under weak stimulation, many neurons may not fire at all, but as the intensity increases, more neurons participate in firing. Therefore, the total potential of the nerve impulse is greater.
2. **The second characteristic is the existence of thresholds.** If the intensity of stimulation at a receptor site is below some minimum, the result may not only be the slowing of neural

firing, but may inhibit all firing. Physical stimulation at a receptor site, below threshold intensity will produce no detectable change in the rate of firing in the sensory nerve.

3. **The third characteristic of receptors and their associated sensory nerves is adaptation.** Again, this is related to the characteristic of individual neurons.

> **Consumption of alcohol and/or drugs will result in:**
> 1. **The slowing of the number of neural firings or cessation of neuron participation.**
> 2. **A rise in the catalytic thresholds of the neural sites**
>   **Or**
> 3. **An increase in the rate of adaptation at the receptor sites.**

The Associators

Associators are structures that are specifically constructed to transmit nerve impulses from the receptors to the Central Nervous System and back to Effectors. Just as muscle cells are specialized for contraction, cells known as neurons are adapted to allow for the conduction of nerve impulses.

An impulse must pass from one neuron to another. For this to occur, it must travel from the dendrites of the cell, to the cell body known as cytoplasm, and continue along the axon to the synaptic junction with yet another neuron (see Figure 3).

The impulse can be superficially compared to the current within an electrical wire. The main obvious difference is, the travel speeds. It can travel at approximately 360 feet per second, while an electrical current travels at the speed of light.

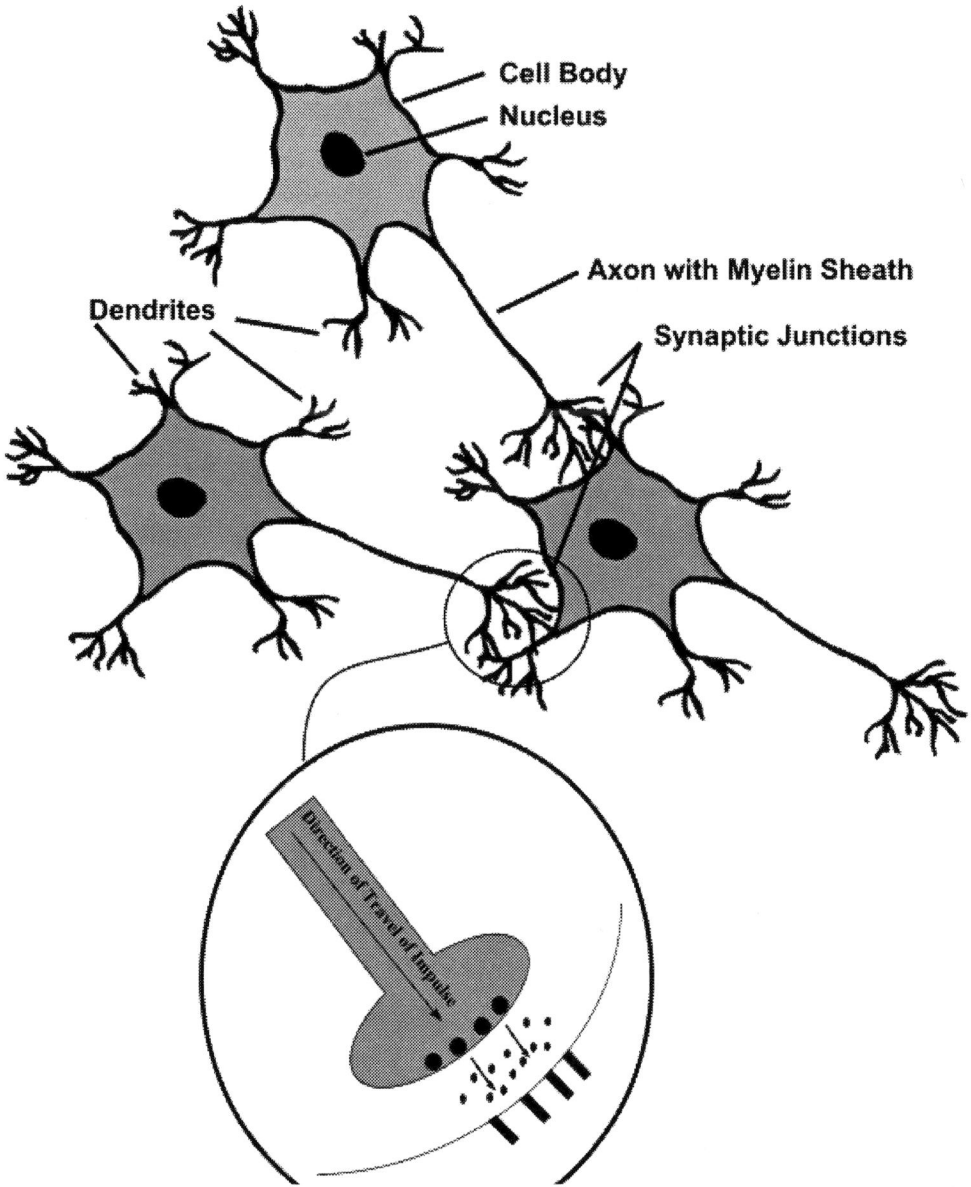

Figure 3: Depiction of a Synaptic Junction

A neuron moves an impulse along by producing a complete chemical depolarization of the cell membrane. It can be likened to a "wave," moving along and passing from one section of the cell to the next. This wave of depolarization constitutes the nerve impulse and is known as its *spike potential*. When a spike potential occurs, it is said to be "firing" with the magnitude of a potential determined by the characteristics of the individual neuron, rather than the stimulation that produced the "firing" in the first place. In other words, if a neuron fires at all, it does so at its maximum intensity, and this maximum varies with the size and type of neuron. Finally, it is important to understand that a nerve impulse moves only in one direction.

> **The mechanism of a neuron, its associated synaptic junctions, and the activity of transmitting impulses from one to the other are certainly not as simplistic as the preceding paragraph would suggest. Many, very complex, scientific factors come into play. Nevertheless, it must be stressed that the entire operation, regardless of the complexity, is altered when alcohol and/or drugs are introduced into the scheme.**
>
> **Alcohol is thought to interfere with the transmission of nerve impulses at the synaptic junction. It exerts a continuous and progressive depression on the Central Nervous System. These changes are manifested as alterations in character, personality and other outward, visible symptoms of a dysfunctional CNS.**

The synaptic junction is a gap of approximately .01 micron or one millionth of a meter. The spike potential of one neuron stimulates the synaptic vesicles at the tip of the axon, causing a secretion of a chemical known as a neurotransmitter. The neurotransmitter, in turn, stimulates the dendrites of a second neuron, thereby producing a "spike potential" in the next neuron.

Neurotransmitters

Neurotransmitters are small protein molecules that are liberated by a pre-synaptic neuron into the synaptic junction, forcing a change in the post synaptic membrane potential of a secondary neuron. They act on receptors by binding to and causing a conformational change in the post-synaptic neuron. This binding and conformal change forces either an opening (excitation) or closing (inhibitory) of the post synaptic receptors.

Neurotransmitters are synthesized in the cell body and are transported to the terminal end of the neuron axon, where they are encapsulated into the terminal vesicles and remain there until activated by a neural impulse. When an action potential occurs, an influx of calcium ions causes the vesicles of the pre-synaptic membrane to open, and the neurotransmitter is released into the junction. Thus, the appropriate message leaves the presynaptic neuron and is transported to the postsynaptic neuron across the synaptic junction.

It should be mentioned that with a few exceptions, the same molecule can function as either an excitor or inhibitor,

Acetylcholine	Most Excitatory
Dopamine	Excitatory and Inhibitory
Epinephrine	Excitatory
Serotonin	Excitatory
Glutamate	Excitatory
Glycine	Most Excitatory
g-Aminobutric Acid (GABA)	Inhibitor

Figure 4: Table of known neurotransmitters

because there are a small number of neurotransmitters, but a great many types and sizes of receptors on a large variety of cells. Acetylcholine, for instance, can act as an excitor when it binds to one type of receptor, and as an inhibitor when bound on another kind.

One of the neurotransmitters playing a major role in addiction is Dopamine. As a chemical messenger, Dopamine is similar to Adrenaline. It affects brain processes that control movement, emotional response and ability to experience pleasure and pain. Cocaine and other drugs of abuse alter the Dopamine function, which force very different actions than is normally expected. The specific action depends on which Dopamine receptors the drugs stimulate or inhibit and how well they mimic Dopamine.

Drugs such as Cocaine and Amphetamine produce their effects by changing the flow of neurotransmitters. They produce affects of observable behavior and heart function in similar ways. Furthermore, both drugs increase the amount of Dopamine in the synapse. Cocaine achieves this action by preventing dopamine reuptake, while Amphetamine helps to release more Dopamine.

GABA (gamma-aminobutyric acid) is the most important inhibitory neurotransmitter in the Central Nervous System. It inhibits the presynaptic release of neurotransmitters. In fact, GABA can be found in 60% to 80% of all CNS neurons. Subtypes of GABA receptors are activated by the mushroom toxin muscimol, which mimics the action of GABA at receptor sites.

Allosteric facilitation of GABA receptors occurs at several distinct sites. These types of compounds are used as sedatives and anxiolytics. They bind the receptor open to indirectly promote GABA binding.

Nerve And Nerve Tracts

Research into the action of Associators most often focuses on groups of neurons that operate together, known as *"neural cables."* A single, isolated, neural fiber will reveal very little about human behavior. When one occurs by itself, in the midst of body masses, it is called a *"nerve."* When it occurs along with other neural tissue, such as the Brain or Spinal Cord, it is called a *"nerve tract."* In either case, it consists of millions of neurons conducting impulses in one-way directions.

Nerves which conduct impulses from the Receptors are known as *"sensory"* or *"afferent nerves."* Those that conduct impulses to the Effectors are known as *"motor"* or *"efferent nerves."* The cell bodies which make up these nerves and tracts are grouped together and are known as *"ganglia"* and *"plexuses,"* or, if they are located within the Brain, ***"nuclei"*** (not to be confused with the nuclei of individual cells).

A nerve impulse takes a normal course to affect a change in the human body from a sensory neuron, through associator neurons, to structure or structures within the brain or spinal cord and lastly, back to a motor neuron. This circular system of neurological action and reaction is said to constitute a ***"Reflex Arc"*** (see Figure 5).

Reflex Arc

A Reflex Arc consists of any hypothetical set of sensory, associator and motor neurons. (In actuality, millions of sensory, associator and motor neurons interact for even the simplest of acts). They are the physiological units of the nervous system and the separate neurons are the anatomical units. The action which results from a nerve impulse passing over a Reflex Arc is called a ***"Reflex."*** It is a response to a stimulus and may or may not be a conscious act.

Reflex Classification

There are several common methods of classifying reflexes.

1. The first categories are based according to the muscles involved in executing a response:

   Simple – a response brought about by the contraction of a single muscle. For example, consider a corneal reflex or the closing of an eyelid, following mechanical stimulation of the surface of the eyeball.

   Coordinated – a response characterized by the contraction of several muscles in a smooth, orderly fashion. For example, walking, typing, etc.

Convulsive – a response characterized by the contraction of several muscles in a jerky, disorderly fashion. For example, seizures.

2. According to the level of the Central Nervous System stimulated, and the consequent action to take place, different neural fibers and macroscopic pathways serve each of these levels.

   a) **First Level** – a response made possible by the function of nerves and spinal cord at a given level. For example, knee jerk or involuntary urination.

   b) **Second Level** – a response made possible by the functioning of nerves, spinal cord and the lower part of the brain; that is, any of its divisions except the cerebrum. For example: walking.

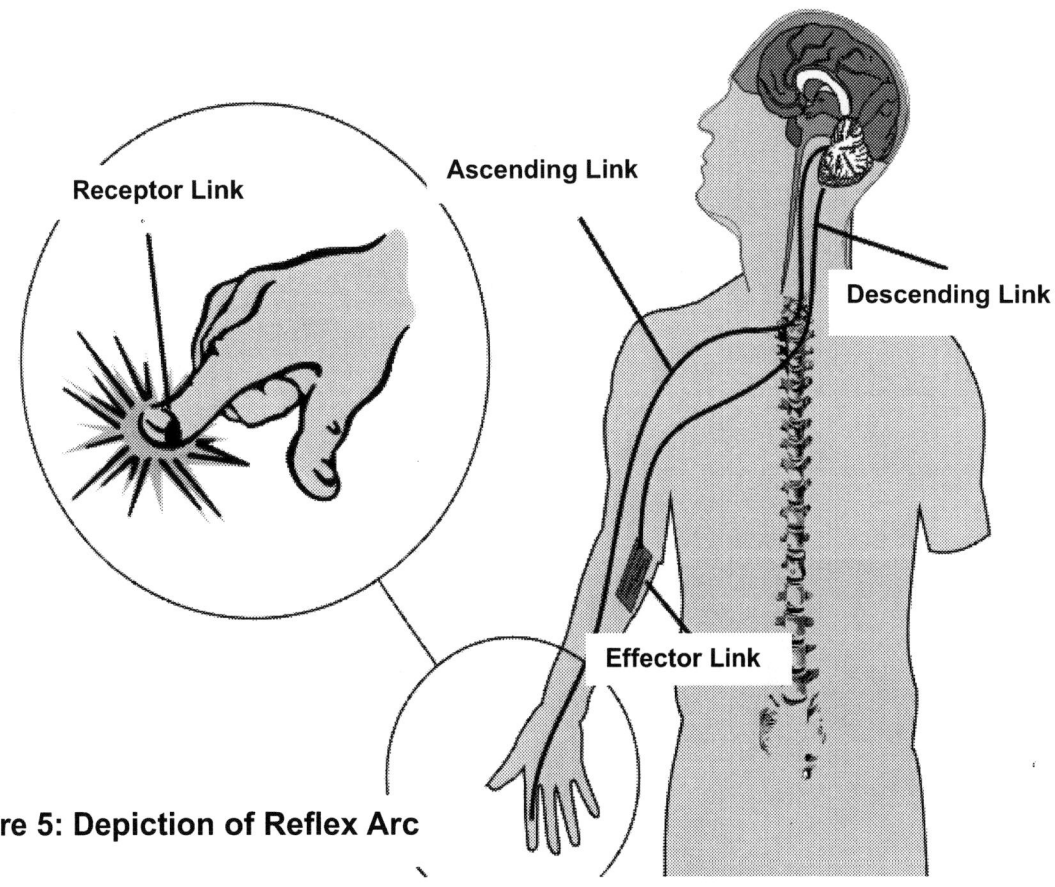

Figure 5: Depiction of Reflex Arc

c) **Third Level** – a response made possible by the functioning of nerves, spinal cord, brain stem and the cerebrum. Examples: any response involving a mental thought process, such as; reasoning, verbal communication, etc.

d) Reflexes are classified according to whether they are **Natural** or **Coordinated.**

Natural Reflex (Inherited, Instinctive, Inborn or Unconditioned) is that response, which naturally results from a given stimulus without previous learning. These reflexes are present at birth. Examples include: newborns sucking or knee jerking.

Conditioned Reflex (Learned or Acquired) is a reflex, which is a response to a stimulus that was originally inadequate to cause a response. Repeated association with an inadequate stimulus however, becomes adequate in and of itself.

Whenever a reflex arc is first used, the nerve impulse is slowed considerably or even blocked completely at the synaptic junction. Repeated use of the arc, however, causes the synapses to offer less and less resistance. From this physiological fact follows the natural law that *repetition is the primary requisite to learning.* Therefore, lower synaptic resistance to the flow of the nerve impulse precipitates all learning and habit formations.

> **By far, the greatest majority of human responses are learned.**

Physicians often try to cause certain reflexes as a means of discovering whether or not the nervous system is in a normal, healthy condition. One of the reflexes, easily and frequently tested, is the knee jerk. Tapping a particular tendon in the knee, when the leg is relaxed and flexed, stimulates receptors in the patellar tendon and its overlaying skin. If the nervous system is normal, the fibers of the stimulated receptors carry the neural impulse via associator neurons to the brain or spinal cord where it is analyzed. It is then shifted to motor neurons which transmit the message back to the extensor muscle of the leg, causing it to contract. Failure of the knee to jerk in response to stimulation indicates injury or illness to either the nerves supplying the leg or of the lumbar region of the cord. Alcohol and/or drugs will force a dysfunction of these processes, thus indicating intoxication.

The Effectors

Generally, the body's environment is influenced in a third way by two functional groups:

- Muscles
- Glands

Muscles

Muscles are the more conspicuous of the two, because they make all bodily movements possible. They are groups or masses cells, which perform their function within the body by contracting. The quality of contractility is possessed, to some degree, by all living cells, but is most highly developed within this the muscle cell.

All muscle tissue possesses the following characteristics:

- **It is contractile** – the cells are able to shorten and thicken themselves.
- **It is irritable** – it responds to various kinds of stimuli, such as mechanical and chemical stimuli.
- **It possesses tone** – healthy muscle is never completely relaxed, but always partially contracted, even at rest.
- **It is extensible** – it can be stretched.
- **It is elastic** – it resumes its original length after the stretching force is removed.

The mechanical change which occurs in a muscle when it contracts is a form of work, and all work requires the expenditure of energy in order to be accomplished. Physiologists have long sought to explain the rapidly available source of energy which makes muscle contractions possible.

Thus far, research has shown that when a stimulus reaches a muscle, an organic phosphate, *Phosphagen*, immediately breaks down into an inorganic phosphate, *Phosphoric Acid*, and another chemical, *Creatine*. When this occurs, a supply of energy is liberated, causing a muscle contraction. The nerve impulse acts as a match that sets off this explosive reaction and occurs during the very brief latent period. This reaction is expressed in equation form as:

Neural Impulse ↔ Phosphagen = Phosphoric Acid + Creatine = Energy

The purpose for describing the above reaction is to show the importance of the neural impulse in causing a chemical reaction and movement of a muscle. If alcohol or drugs of any kind inhibit the impulse, the muscle will not function as intended. This becomes obvious when an intoxicated subject attempts to accomplish a Field Sobriety Test.

There are three types of muscles:

1. **Skeletal** (also known as Striated or Voluntary)
2. **Smooth**
3. **Cardiac**

Skeletal Muscles

Skeletal muscles control all body movements. They are elongated, tubular structures with as many as several hundred nuclei. These muscles are directly stimulated by the nervous system and characterized by their ability to react in quick and deliberate movements. Each motor neuron that leaves the spinal cord usually enervates many other different muscle fibers. The number is dependent on the type and usage of the involved muscle.

Fine Motor Control: These types of muscles react rapidly and possess properties far more exacting than those of other muscle tissues types. Fingers, for example, have relatively few muscle fibers located within them, but have a large number of nerves attached. This necessitates many thousands of synaptic junctions in just one finger alone. Alcohol, depressants and stimulants have a detrimental effect on the synaptic acetylcholine. This results in slowing and/or stopping the reaction between the axial end of the neuron and the dendrital filaments of the next consecutive neuron. Consequently, larger numbers of synaptic junctions are affected, and affectation of fine motor control musculature is apparent much sooner than with ordinary skeletal muscles.

> **Note: It is apparent that alcohol and other drugs will affect fine motor control muscle groupings before large muscle groupings.**

Smooth Muscles

Smooth muscles operate many of the internal organs. They appear as spindle-shaped, uninuclear cells and are located in the walls of internal organs. By their synchronous action, food is propelled through the digestive system, urine is transported from the kidneys, blood flow and blood pressure is regulated, etc.

Cardiac Muscles

The Cardiac muscle provides continuous, rhythmic contractions of the heart. It is constructed somewhat like a composite of skeletal and smooth muscles. They contract automatically, like smooth muscles, but are striated and multinucleated, like skeletal muscles.

Glands

Glands control routine bodily functions and also play a part in emotion as well as energizing of various aspects of human behavior.

There are two general types of glands:

1. Duct Glands
2. Endocrine Glands

Duct Glands

Duct Glands produce secretions which pass through ducts into body cavities (Digestive Juices) or to the outside of the body (Perspiration).

Endocrine Glands

Endocrine glands produce secretions, which are passed into the blood stream and control vital bodily functions and some behaviors. They are anatomically distinguished from the more numerous duct glands in that they have no ducts and secrete directly into the blood stream. Their locations within the body, therefore, are of little functional significance. A hormone released into the blood stream at any point in or on the body will be rapidly distributed throughout.

> **The glandular physiological action of the body is severely inhibited by the introduction of alcohol and narcotic drugs.**

HUMAN INTELLECT AND REASONING

In this section, the Central Nervous System and its associated structures have been described in general terms. The manner in which neural impulses are transmitted to and from the CNS has also been portrayed. Coordination of these human systems allows for cognitive thought processes to take place and the human intellect to exist.

As mentioned, there are distinct functional divisions between the cerebrospinal and the autonomic systems. They are however, integrated by the brain and indeed, fuel each other, much as the electrical and mechanical systems of a motor vehicle. This integration of conscious and unconscious stimuli is a complex phenomenon carried out by nerve cells located within the Central Nervous System. These cells are arranged in neural cables, as well as nerve tracts, forming billions of different circuits. This system, allows us to be **"sentient beings."** We are conscious of many thoughts and stimuli simultaneously, possessing the ability to reason and understand, and to imagine and create. Remember, there are seventeen (17) billion or more different synaptic junctions, or circuits connected with literally millions of different cables and tracts. One can only imagine the ability of the CNS to carry out an incredible number of different functions at the same time.

The human intellect allows the human being to **"reason."** Most classical philosophers view "reasoning" as a biological instrument that enables us to make practical adjustments to our environment and/or ourselves. It allows for the survival of the human species. It empowers us with creative thought, memory, motor skills, perceptions, feelings and all the other aspects of the human experience.

Certain highly engineered mechanical systems are constructed to perform both generalized and specific functions. They are, nevertheless, composed of unique but interdependent subsystems. An automobile must have ball-bearings in order to roll. At the same time, the machine which manufactures ball bearings must have bearings itself. So too, the CNS is constructed of specialized, interacting divisions and subdivisions, and as incredible as it seems, this marvelous and intricate organization works perfectly, until….alcohol, depressants, and/or stimulant drugs are introduced into the overall scheme.

So far, a picture of the Central Nervous System has been presented as a complicated arrangement of pathways for getting sensory impulses from the receptors to the various sensory and analyzation areas of the cerebral cortex and then to the muscles, and glands. Further, the cerebral cortex, having the ability to create new and exciting thought through the intellect, transmits the thought processes over the same circuits and in the same manner as the typical reflex arc. Therefore, given this arrangement, it is reasonable to analyze behavior in terms of the relationship between the sensory impulses going to the brain and the motor impulses leaving it. Such an analysis is made in terms of stimulus and response. A stimulus is the input that arouses a receptor, in or on the human body, and a response is a specific item of behavior caused by the receptor stimulation. The basic unit of behavior consists of a stimulus, producing an impulse that passes along a sensory nerve, up the spinal cord to the brain and back along a motor nerve to an Effector. This being the case, all behaviors consist of a stimuli and a response.

With few exceptions, drugs are utilized by the human body to prevent or cure illness, or allow the body to heal itself. Alcohol and drugs have a valid social, physiological and psychological reason for existing; however, when alcohol and impairing drugs are introduced into the human body and the person attempts to operate a motor vehicle, a tragic outcome occurs. This is because the impairment occurs at the molecular level of the neurotransmitter. The drugs either inhibit or enhance the chemical responses, forcing incredible transformations of personality, intellect and mechanical abilities.

Ideally, those who consume a drug should voluntarily exempt themselves from driving; however, because human beings all too often refuse to understand the incredible liabilities or consequences for their actions, laws have been enacted to sanction those who violate Driving Under the Influence statutes.

> **Does a man or woman need "reason," in order to operate a motor vehicle? The answer is a resounding YES. They must be able to "make practical adjustments" to accommodate the ever changing environment in which they are operating their vehicles. Alcohol and/or drugs deny or at least slow this crucial ability to "reason."**

CHAPTER TWO: IMPAIRING DRUGS

SECTION ONE: Pharmacology and Toxicology of Drugs

PHARMACOLOGY

Pharmacology is the study or the science of drugs, their sources, physiochemical properties, biological effects and therapeutic uses. It is the examination of drugs with respect to:
- Mode of actions
- Side effects
- Toxicity
- Range of dosage
- Rate and route of excretion
- Individual differences in responses, such as:
  - Idiosyncratic or Allergic Reactions
  - Interactions with other drugs.

Pharmacognosy and Pharmacodynamics

The science of Pharmacology is commonly divided into two major fields of interest:
- **Pharmacognosy**
  and
- **Pharmacodynamics**

Pharmacognosy is the study of crude drugs and the plants from which they are procured.

Pharmacodynamics is the analysis of the effects of drugs on living tissues and the inherent changes in biological function produced by drugs. It deals with the absorption of drugs and their distribution throughout the human body. This science researches those chemical transformations precipitated by ingested drugs and their eventual elimination or excretion.

TOXICOLOGY

Toxicology is the study or science of the poisonous effects of drugs.

There are certain general facts that apply to the Pharmacology and Toxicology of all drugs:
- In therapeutic doses, all drugs exhibit some type of **Pharmacognosy and Pharmacodynamics** effects in all human beings, all of the time.
- All drugs exhibit, to a greater or lesser degree, certain side effects. These effects are spoken of as toxic reactions, and act as tissue contaminants.
- The degree of damage inflicted upon the human tissue is largely a product of:
  - The dose consumed
  - The period of time over which the drug is administered
- The magnitude of the response produced by a drug is proportional to the dose for an adult. In other words, the actual dose employed must be adjusted to individual circumstances.
  - For example, some individuals will be unusually sensitive to the effects of certain drugs. The therapeutic dosage, therefore, must be adjusted and in some circumstances, the drug should not be administered.

Forensic Toxicology

Forensic toxicology is a discipline of science concerned with the study of toxic substances or poisons, of which there are many thousands.

The first comprehensive work on forensic toxicology was published in 1813 by Mathieu Orifila. He was a respected Spanish chemist and the physician who is often given the distinction of "Father of Toxicology." His work emphasized the need for adequate proof of identification and the need for quality assurance. It also recognized the application of forensic toxicology in pharmaceutical, clinical, industrial and environmental fields.

Currently, forensic toxicology is the study of alcohol, drugs (licit and illicit,) and poisons, including their composition, preparations and identification. It includes research into the absorption, distribution and elimination characteristics of such substances in the body, as well as the manner in which the body responds to their presence and the factors which determine drug safety and effectiveness. To understand drug action one must know where and how the effects occur in the body (See Chapter One).

The main concept of this training manual will deal with the science of Forensic Toxicology; however, because of the complexity of this subject, the science of pharmacology will play a large role in explaining the effects and affects of alcohol and other impairing drugs.

SECTION TWO: Drug Effects on the Central Nervous System

Pleasure, which scientists call reward, is a very powerful biological force for our survival. If a person does something that is pleasurable, the brain is wired in such a way that the pleasurable act is repeated. Life-sustaining activities, such as eating, activate a circuit of specialized nerve cells devoted to producing and regulating pleasure. One important set of these nerve cells, which uses a chemical neurotransmitter called dopamine, sits at the top of the brain-stem in the Ventral Tegmental Area (VTA). These dopamine-containing neurons relay messages about pleasure through their nerve fibers to cells in a limbic system structure called the Nucleus Accumbens. Other fibers reach to a related part of the frontal region of the cerebral cortex. The pleasure circuit, which is known as the Mesolimbic Dopamine System, spans the survival oriented brain-stem, the emotional limbic system and the frontal cerebral cortex. DUI driving offenses are directly related to the pleasure/reward system of the human body.

Definition: Drug

A drug is broadly defined as any substance that can alter the homeostasis or chemical balance of the body. This definition includes a wide variety of substances, from antibiotics to the most powerful psychotropic drugs, such as Morphine and Haldol. The emphasis of this training manual, however, is obviously focused on those drugs that cause impairment of the ability to safely operate a motor vehicle.

Impairing Drugs

Definition: Drug Misuse And Abuse

Drug misuse is the consumption of a drug, which will result in transient physical, mental or social problems. Drug abuse is the use of a substance that will result in long-term physical, mental or social problems. The use of any impairing substance that affects the ability to drive a motor vehicle, while in fact operating a motor vehicle, is both a misuse, an abuse and is criminally negligent.

Trends

Prescription Drugs

The National Institute on Drug Abuse has conducted extensive research into the prescription drug misuse and abuse arena and reported some rather disturbing news. Several indicators suggest that prescription drug abuse is on the rise in the United States. In 1998, an estimated 1.6 million Americans used prescription pain relievers non-medically. This is a 181% increase over the time period of 1990 to 1998. Tranquilizer misuse increased an astonishing 132%, and those using stimulant drugs increased 165%. Clearly, almost 2% of the total American population was utilizing impairing prescription drugs in an unlawful manner. This percentage does not take into account those who were using prescription drugs appropriately. These are staggering statistics, and should make the DUI investigator take pause when thought of in the context that nearly 5% or more of the population are currently taking impairing drugs and operating motor vehicles.

Prescription Drugs – Older Adults

The misuse of prescription drugs may be the most common form of drug abuse among the elderly. Elderly persons use prescription medications approximately 3 times as frequently as the general population and have been found to have the poorest rates of compliance with directions for taking a medication.

Prescription Drugs – Adolescents and Young Adults

Data indicates that the most dramatic increase in prescription drug use for non-medical purposes is in the 12 to 25 year olds. Narcotic painkillers and stimulants are the two primary drugs used by the 12 to 17 year-old population.

It also appears that college students' use of Percodan and Vicodin are increasing steadily. Their use of tranquilizers for non-medical reasons has increased by 102%.

Cerebral Cortex – Cerebrum (Including the Thalamus)

Drugs that depress the cellular activity in the cerebrum, such as opiates, barbiturates and alcohol, decrease the acuity of perception and sensation, and decrease alertness, concentration and significantly raise the level of euphoria. This increase in the cellular activity within the cortex causes more vivid impulses to be received, resulting in euphoria, uncoordinated muscle activity and the possibility of hallucinations.

SYSTEMIC INTERACTIONS

Information regarding pleasure and pain is received via the Thalamus, which is the relay center of the brain. All sensory and motor impulses pass through this organ. It can relay signals from the brain stem to all parts of the cerebral cortex and cause a generalized activation of the entire cerebrum. It is also the center for sensations, such as agreeableness and disagreeableness of any given situation. Depression or stimulation of the Thalamus, such as occurs with opiates, tranquilizers or ephedrine-based chemicals will block unpleasant sensations to the cortex and greatly inflate euphoria.

Hypothalamus

The hypothalamus contains the centers that regulate body temperature, hunger, satiety pleasure and pain and is linked directly to the autonomic nervous system. Depressants acting on the neural synapses within this organ cause a person to become drowsy. Stimulant drugs act on the Hypothalamus to increase the activity of the satiety and pleasure centers.

Reticular Activating System

The reticular activating system receives input from all parts of the sensory system as well as from the cerebrum. The major function of the RTS is to control the arousal level of the brain. Depressants decrease the activity of the organ and produce sedation and loss of consciousness. Stimulants force a person to feel alert and euphoric. Very often the function of sensation becomes extremely distorted by LSD and Cannabis.

Cerebellum

The cerebellum controls balance and coordination of various body movements. It is also the center for muscle coordination, tone and the body's equilibrium. Depressants force obvious incoordination in body movement and balance. Stimulants cause tremors.

Medulla Oblongata

The medulla oblongata in the brain stem is the center for such vital functions as respiration, coughing, vomiting and cardiac/vasomotor control. This organ may cease to function, resulting in death, if high levels of depressants are consumed. Stimulants can force uncontrollable activity in the vital functions of the body, also resulting in death.

Factors Affecting Drug Action

Many factors must be considered relative to the effect of drug action on the body.

- First, different drugs exert different effects on various body cells, and unless a substance is able to exert an influence on some body cell or process, no reaction to the substance will take place.
- Second, before a drug enters the body, three important factors will affect the response of the person to the drug. Specifically, its **dose**, the **time it takes to be effective** and the **route of administration**.

There are other factors as well, such as the:
- Individual's Psychological Environment
- Metabolic Rate
- Elimination Route
- Age
- Weight
- Sex

   and
- Hereditary Influences.

The interaction of a drug on the body depends upon:
- Its interaction with a cell body

  and
- The function of that cell in the body.

In some cases, after a drug enters the body, it must be chemically altered before it is able to exert any effect on the body cells. As mentioned in Chapter 1, Section 1, drugs act on the cell at the receptor site in the following ways:
- Increase Activity of the Cell
- Decrease Activity of the Cell
- Block Activity of the Cell
- Replace Missing Components Needed by the Cell
- Aid in Transferring Substances Through Cell Membrane

Dose

The response of the human body to all drugs differs in intensity and effect according to the dose (amount) of a drug consumed. Most drugs do not show an effect until a certain minimal level of the substance is obtained. The lowest dosage of a drug to show an effect on the body is the threshold dosage of the drug. As a result of heredity, different people respond in different ways to the same dosage of a drug; therefore, the dose of a drug required to produce an effective response in 50% of all individuals tested is called the median lethal dose.

The more drug consumed, the stronger the drug effect. For example: In the case of alcohol, an increase in the dose intensifies the negative reactions of the drug, but does not increase the desired effect of euphoria sought by the user. Likewise, an increase in the dosage of penicillin for a bacterial infection will not cure the infection any quicker than the appropriate dose.

Time

The time that it takes for a drug to exert its desired effect once it has entered the body is also important. Some drugs act immediately upon entering the circulatory system. Others may take hours or even days and weeks to manifest a desired effect.

Route of Administration

A very important factor influencing the reaction of drugs within the body is the method by which it is administered.

Oral

Perhaps the most common way of taking drugs is orally. Obviously, this is the most convenient method to consume a drug. Oral consumption also allows digestion to modify a drug, which might be too powerful or too fast acting if administered directly into the bloodstream. Once in the stomach, some drugs, such as alcohol, can go directly into the bloodstream without further digestion. Most are absorbed into the circulatory system along with glucose, amino acids, minerals and vitamins, after being passed into the large or small intestine.

Drugs that are soluble in lipids (fats), such as barbiturates and THC, remain longer in the body. Water-soluble drugs, such as alcohol, tend to be excreted relatively quickly.

Inhalation

Anesthetics, solvents, marijuana and some forms of stimulants are inhaled through the mouth. Cocaine and some forms of amphetamine are inhaled through the nose, where they are absorbed through the mucous membranes in the nostrils. Because the lungs have large beds of capillaries, inhaled chemicals are capable of crossing the membranes to enter the blood fairly rapidly.

Injection

Injection is a common form of administration for drugs, particularly with opiates, cocaine and heroin. Drugs taken by injection can be intravenously, intramuscularly or subcutaneously administered. In intravenous injections, the drug can go directly into the circulatory system and act immediately. This is extremely dangerous when administering street drugs, due to the impurities found in these compounds, errors in dosage, bubbles in the syringe and infections from puncturing the skin and vein. Intramuscular injections can also be fairly easily absorbed.

SECTION THREE: Ethyl Alcohol

Physical evidence of wine dating from c. 5000 B.C. has been found in the remains of an ancient pottery jar found in 1968 in Hajji Firuz Tepe, Iran. Residue in the jar contains two characteristic ingredients of wine, specifically, tartaric acid and calcium tartrate.

By 800 B.C. the Chinese knew how to distill a beverage from rice beer and arrack was distilled in the East Indies from sugarcane and rice. The Arabs developed a distillation method that was used to produce a distilled beverage from wine. Greek philosophers reported a crude distillation method, and the Romans apparently produced distilled beverages. Production of distilled spirits was reported in Britain before the Roman conquest. Spain, France and the rest of Western Europe probably produced distilled spirits at an earlier date, but production was apparently limited until the 8th century, after contact with the Arab nations.

Since the latter part of the 18th century, drinking has been a focus of disagreement, sometimes amounting to political warfare among subgroups making up larger national societies. This is so characteristic of a modern complex society troubled by the lack of consensus around many issues of right and wrong or proper and improper behavior.

Within the general category of chemicals known as "alcohol" are different, individual compounds known as Ethyl, Methyl, Butyl and Amyl, etc. Each of these substances is metabolized by the human body into different byproducts; consequently, each has differing levels of toxicity. All of them will cause driving impairment and death if a sufficient quantity is consumed. Ethyl

Alcohol is the only variation of this chemical group to be discussed in this manual.

Ethyl Alcohol is a colorless, almost odorless liquid, completely soluble in water. The human body has an extremely high water content, and alcohol readily enters every cell and tissue (except adipose tissue) of the body. Alcohol is less dense than water and evaporates at a lower temperature.

Alcohol is an "over-the-counter" drug that works by modifying the GABA receptors as well as the receptors utilizing dopamine, seratonin and acetacholine. Additionally, it is toxic to nerve cells and exerts systemic effects by liquefying nerve membranes, just as any solvent would melt plastics. It also acts upon the opiate receptors of the body through its first metabolite, acetaldehyde, which combines with dopamine to form tetrahydroisoquinonolone (TIQ). This interaction with opiate receptors is responsible for the euphoric sensation of alcohol intoxication.

The consumption of alcohol causes marked changes in human behavior. Even low doses significantly impair judgment and coordination, induce feelings of relaxation and tranquility, and suppress anxiety and causes over-confidence.

Fermentation Production Process

Fermentation is the process whereby complex organic molecules are broken down into simpler compounds by the introduction of an enzyme catalyst. The sugars, used as an enzymatic catalyst in the fermentation process, are formed by decomposition of the starches found in corn, potatoes, rice or grain by the introduction of malts and yeast's.

This procedure forms a basic alcohol concentration, which cannot exceed 12% to 14%, because the fermentation process is slowed and stopped by the natural production of the alcohol, which has an antagonistic effect on the process itself.

Distillation Production Process

The process known as distillation increases the alcohol concentration to as high as 95% pure. It is the method used to separate liquids of differing volatility and to purify liquids contaminated with nonvolatile properties. For example, some chemicals have lower boiling temperatures than others. When a mixture containing two or more chemicals with differing boiling points is heated, the chemical with the lower boiling point vaporizes before the other. The purer chemicals are then collected and allowed to cool back to a liquid state within a condenser. The chemicals have been separated without corrupting either solution. For example, Ethyl Alcohol has a lower boiling point (78.3^0 C) than the water (100^0 C) within which it is contained. Consequently, when the mixture is heated, the alcohol vaporizes before the water and is collected and condensed back into a liquid, nearly free of water, or 95% pure. Anhydrous Alcohol (absolute alcohol or 99.9% pure) is produced by additional distillation, with a small amount of the chemical, Benzene.

Medical Usages

Ethyl Alcohol is the only alcohol used extensively in the production of medicine. It was formerly thought to be a remedy for

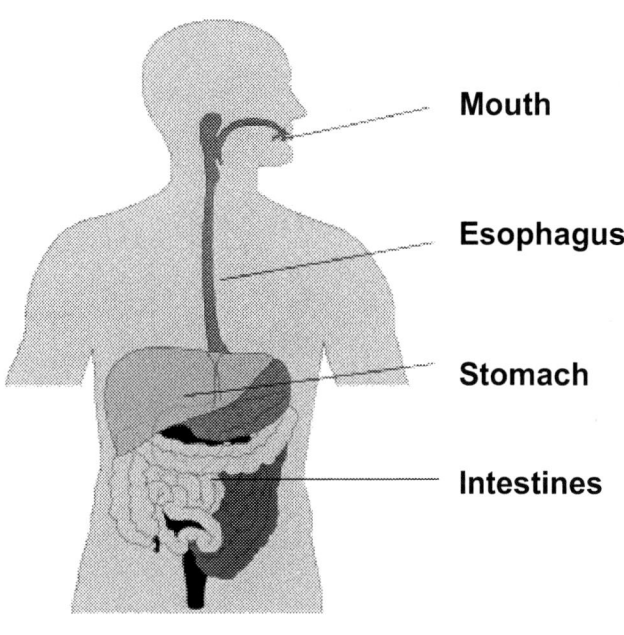

Figure 6: Absorption

Tic Douloureux – is a neuralgia or paroxysmal pain, usually beginning in middle-life and most frequently in women. It is characterized by an intense stabbing pain, which strikes one, or a combination of three facial branches supplied by the trigeminal (fifth cranial) nerve. ETOH is sometimes injected into the facial area to desensitize the nerve fibers and relieve the pain associated with the severe and protracted neurological disorder. Novocain is sometimes substituted.

Methyl Alcohol Poisoning – Ethyl Alcohol is used in the treatment of "Wood Alcohol Poisoning." It attaches chemically to the molecules of Methanol and aids in the natural elimination of the poison.

> **The medical profession utilizes Ethyl Alcohol in many other applications; however, it must be emphasized that the ingestion of Ethyl Alcohol for medical purposes, should be prescribed and closely monitored by a physician. Further, as most state laws reflect, the fact that a drug has been medically prescribed does not relieve the driver, who has consumed one of these drugs, of the liability and/or culpability for driving while impaired.**

> **Cold remedies should be a major concern of DUI investigators. A person who consumes one of these "cold remedies" can become significantly impaired. Within these compounds, a relatively low alcohol concentration, 10% to 37%, is mixed with an antihistamine, which is impairing in itself. This combination causes a synergistic effect, which manifests itself by obvious symptomology of impairment greater than the cumulative sum of two or more drugs when combined.**

Impairing Drugs

Alcoholic Beverages

Ethyl Alcohol is also the only alcohol used to prepare alcoholic beverages. These drinks contain alcohol concentrations of 4% to 50% and more. The following are some of the different types of beverages produced commercially:

Whiskey & Bourbon – Is obtained by the distillation of the fermented mash of wholly or partially malted cereal grains and contains 40% to 50% Ethyl Alcohol.

Brandy – Is obtained by the distillation of the fermented juice of grapes and contains approximately 50% Ethyl Alcohol.

Wine – Wine is obtained by the fermentation of grapes or other fruits and contains various acids such as tartaric, tannic or malic. It contains approximately 12% ETOH.

Beer – Is obtained by fermentation of yeasts, grains and malts. It contains approximately 4% ETOH.

Absorption

When consumed, alcohol is absorbed into the blood through the mucous lining of the upper gastrointestinal tract (mouth, esophagus, stomach and small intestine). The rate of absorption varies among the different organs.

Absorption from the mouth is very slow, from the stomach somewhat faster, and very rapid from the upper end of the small intestine. By the time the fluid gets to the large intestine, the alcohol has been completely absorbed.

The rate of absorption, through the stomach lining and the passage to the remainder of the gastrointestinal tract can vary due to several factors:

- **The type of alcoholic beverage consumed** – If the concentration is high, it can irritate the stomach and the intestinal lining and slow the rate of absorption.
- **Whether or not carbonated beverages were mixed with the alcohol** – Carbonated beverages tend to speed up the absorption rate.
- **Whether or not fatty or oily beverages were consumed with the alcohol** – Fatty or oily beverages slow the absorption rate.
- **The amount and type of food consumed in conjunction with the alcohol** – Food eaten during the consumption of alcohol will mix with the beverage and slow the rate of absorption.
- **Altitude** – The higher the altitude, the faster the absorption.

Generally speaking, all alcohol will be absorbed into the blood stream from 30 to 90 minutes after the last drink. It is commonly felt that the ETOH is absorbed at an average of 45 minutes.

> **The concentration of alcohol is directly proportional to the body water content. Within the context already discussed, the concentration will vary according to the body weight. In other words, a larger male must consume more alcohol to attain the same alcohol concentration as a smaller male.**

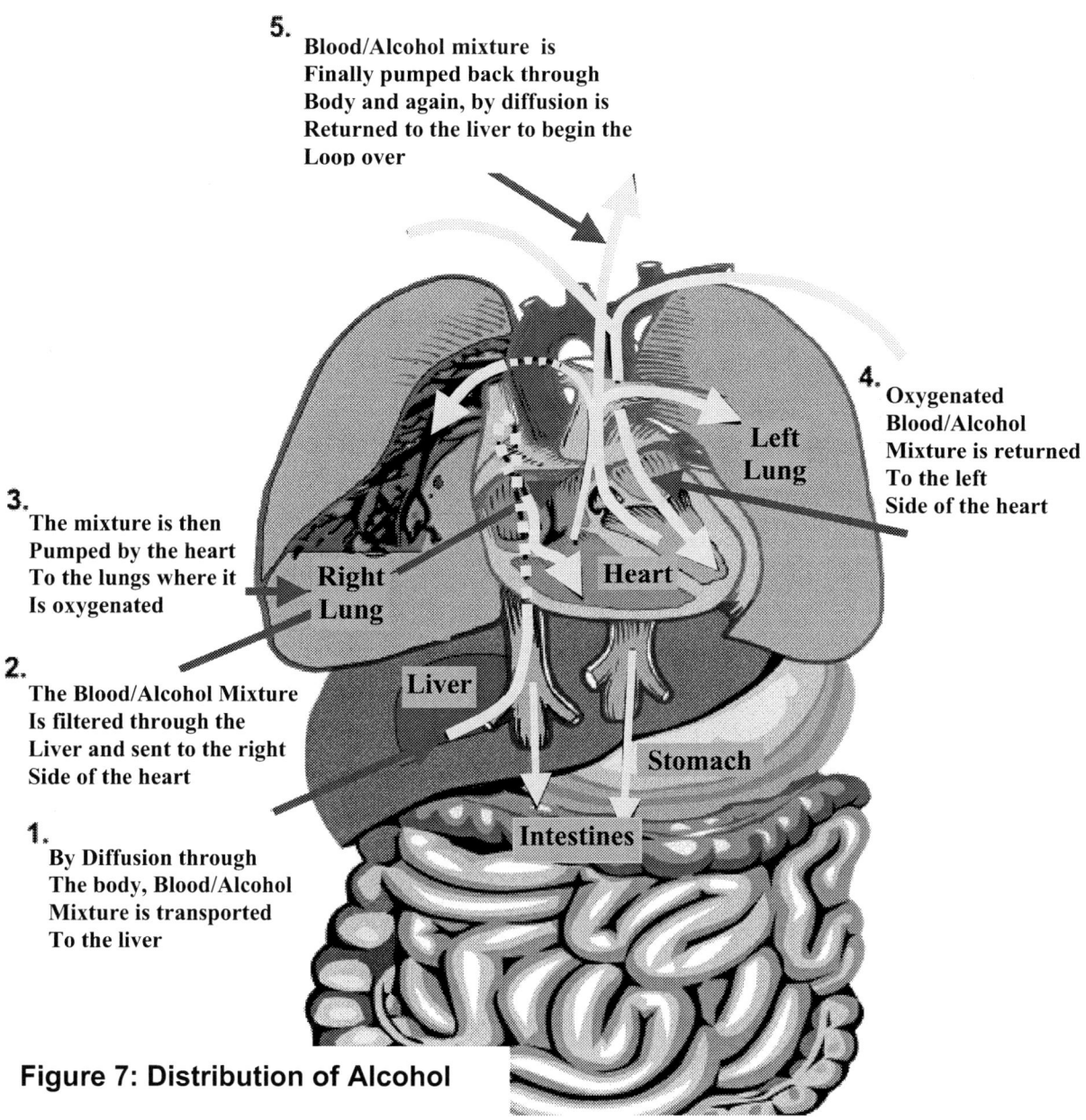

Figure 7: Distribution of Alcohol

Distribution

Once the gastrointestinal tract has absorbed the alcohol, it is transported throughout the entire body via the vascular system (see Figure 7).

- It is first moved to and passed through the liver.
- From the liver, the alcohol-enriched blood is moved to and passed through the right side of the heart.
- The mixture is then pumped to and filtered through the lungs and returned to the left side of the heart.
- At this point, the blood-alcohol combination leaves the heart, and is distributed throughout the remainder of the entire body.
- This process is repeated over and over again, until the alcohol has been eliminated.

During absorption and distribution phases, ethanol is distributed into the tissues of the body in approximately the same ratio as its water content. Those parts of the body rich in water (blood plasma, urine, brain, kidney, and liver) become correspondingly rich in alcohol, while those parts which contain little water, such as bone or fat, attract much less alcohol.

Gender Differences

Males are approximately 70% water, while females have approximately 55% water. Regardless of gender however, an obese person has less water per pound of body weight than a thin person, due to the higher percentage of adipose tissue (fat). This accounts for the fact that females have less water content than males, because of the additional adipose tissue located within the breasts, buttocks and thighs. For example, compare a 200-pound male with a 100-pound male. The 200-pound male has approximately 140 pounds of water, and the 100-pound male has approximately 70 pounds of water. If each person consumes 1 ounce of Ethyl Alcohol, the 100-pound male will have a higher concentration of alcohol than the 200-pound male. That is to say, there will be more alcohol per pound of water, in the 100 pound than the 200-pound male.

Compare a 100-pound male with a 100-pound female. The male has approximately 70 pounds of water while the female has 55 pounds of water. Again, if each consumes 1 ounce of ETOH, the female will have a higher concentration than the male. The female will have more alcohol, per pound of water, than the male.

Weight to Volume

Alcohol concentrations within the human body are expressed as a function of weight to volume. For example, a breath test reveals a weight of alcohol (GRAMS) per volume (LITERS). The % symbol, as used in toxicology reports or breath measurement device records, is a shorthand notation, meaning grams of ethanol, per 100 milliliters of blood, 210 liters of breath, or 67 milliliters of urine.

Examples:

.10% = .10 grams of ethanol/1hundred ML of blood.

.10% = .10 grams of ethanol/210 L of breath air.

.10% = .10 grams of ethanol/67 ML of urine.

Blood Alcohol Calculations

The BAC levels on a toxicology report supplied by a hospital laboratory are often expressed in the form of mg/ml. These representations are the same as those received from a breath measurement device, but expressed differently. Conversion of these factors is accomplished by the following:

$$.8 \text{ mg/ml} = 80 \text{ mg} = .08\%$$

The following mathematical formulas are supplied so that an investigating Officer can write a more insightful and more professional report of the DUI incident. Within the report and while testifying in a court of law, if the Officer is able to specifically state the amount of Ethanol in the subject's system, he or she will have progressed a long way in advancing their professional image as an expert DUI investigator.

Widmark Formula

1. To Determine Blood Alcohol Content

The Widmark Formula is one of the earliest methods used to determine the Blood Alcohol Content of a subject.

$$BAC = \frac{OzETOH \times .05 \times 150}{BW}$$

In order to obtain the BAC, the investigator must know the number of ounces of ETOH consumed by the subject and the subject's body weight. It is generally found that a subject will not be able or willing to supply this information, however. Point of fact, in most instances, the BAC will be revealed when the result of a breath measurement device is printed out, or a toxicology report is returned from the crime lab.

The information most needed by an investigator, in order to compile a descriptive report is:

- The number of ounces of pure Ethyl Alcohol present in a subject's body

and

- The amount of Alcoholic Beverage present in a subject's body.

---

2. To Determine The Ounces of Pure Alcohol

Example: A breath measurement device shows that a subject has a BAC of .24% and the subject weighs 200 pounds.

$$OzETOH = \frac{BAC}{.10} \times 2 \times \frac{BW}{150}$$

$$OzETOH = \frac{.24}{.10} \times 2 \times \frac{200}{150}$$

$$OzETOH = 2.4 \times 2 \times 1.3$$

$$OzETOH = 6.39$$

As demonstrated, the amount of ETOH within an individual's body can certainly be calculated; unfortunately, this figure may not mean much to a jury of average citizens. For example, there is a perception that 6.39 ounces of Ethyl Alcohol does not seem like too much for a 200-pound man. It would be much more beneficial if the investigator could portray to a court the amount of alcoholic beverage actually consumed; therefore, the following formula can be used.

3. To Determine the Number of Drinks of Alcoholic Beverage

$$OzBev = \frac{BAC}{.10} \times 2 \times \frac{100}{proof} \times 2 \times \frac{BW}{150}$$

$$OzBev = \frac{24}{.10} \times 2 \times \frac{100}{8} \times 2 \times \frac{200}{150}$$

$$OzBev = 2.4 \times 2 \times 12.5 \times 2 \times 1.34$$

$$OzBev = 160.8$$

160.8 ounces corresponds to 13.4, 12-ounce cans of beer.

If the same individual as before, with a BAC of .24% and weighing 200 pounds, is factored into the above formula, a number representing the actual numbers of drinks can be determined. In this particular case, the beverage consumed is beer, which is approximately 4% Ethyl Alcohol, or 8 proof.

Impairing Drugs

Demonstrating to a court of law that the subject had 13.4, 12 oz. cans of beer in their system, at the time of the chemical test, is certainly more dramatic and factual than simply stating the BAC amount, or even the number of ounces of pure alcohol.

Extrapolation

Webster's New World Dictionary defines extrapolation as, **"the estimation of something unknown based on known facts."** Applying this principle to a DUI investigation, it is possible to estimate a subject's BAC from known facts, even though the breath, blood or urine sample was taken after the fact.

Most State DUI laws indicate that if a blood, breath or urine sample is taken within two hours of the offense, the Blood Alcohol Concentration (BAC), indicated by the breath measurement device or toxicology report, is adjudged to be the same as when the offense occurred. If the chemical test is taken more than two hours after the alleged driving or actual physical control, the trier of facts shall determine the weight, given the results of the test. This means, that if a chemical test was taken after the two-hour limit, the results can still be admitted in a court of law; however, the

> **NOTE: A blood alcohol concentration does not equate to the extent of impairment.**

Professional Police Officers can do better. The BAC at the time of the offense can still be determined, even though the time has elapsed. If qualified by a court, an expert can testify to an opinion. In the case of DUI Blood Alcohol Concentrations, the investigator will be able to testify as to his or her opinion of a BAC at the time of the offense. This is accomplished by extrapolating back from the time the sample was taken to the point in time at which the offense took place. The only information needed is the approximate weight of the subject and the time when he or she last consumed an alcoholic beverage.

In addition, an investigator must have enough (in the opinion of the court) skill and experience with the previously described mathematical equations; however, no requirement exists as to how that skill or experience was obtained. An accredited course of scientific study or training is not always essential. Courts can accept a background of practical experience in a variety of areas, instead of a course of scientific study or training.

The trial judge first determines competency in regard to skill or experience. After a proper foundation, as to the validity of the science is established, along with a proffer of experience, skill and knowledge, the officer will be able to offer an opinion as to the level of a BAC at the time of the offense.

The calculations are completed at any time after the initial investigation and are accomplished by:

Step 1. Obtain a BAC by the use of a breath measurement device, a blood test or a urine test.

Step 2. Establish, as closely as possible, the time of the alleged driving or actual physical control, and then determine the length of time since that situation occurred.

Step 3. Multiply .015% by the time period elapsed.

Step 4. Add the product of step 3 to the BAC received from a chemical test.

Example: A car-pole traffic accident occurs at 0100 hours. and the driver flees. The subject is located at 0500 hours. The subject displays characteristics of intoxication and you can establish (ask the subject) that no alcohol has been consumed since the accident. The subject is arrested for DUI, Hit and Run, and Failure to Maintain Control of a Motor Vehicle. He or she is taken to the station and a breath test shows that the BAC of .14%.

Remember, on average, an individual will metabolize 1/3 ounce or .015% of Ethyl Alcohol per hour. Determine the number of ounces present at 0100 hours given the .14% determined at 0500 hours. Keep in mind that 4 hours has elapsed since the accident. Therefore, 4 X .015% = .06%. Added to .14%, it is found that the individual's BAC at the time of the accident was .20%. Remember, the court has the right to determine the "weight" of such evidence. Nevertheless, if the investigator clearly and concisely, with the assistance of the prosecutor, articulates the evidence and the basis for the opinions, there should be little problem getting the evidence admitted into the record.

The courts may cause the investigating Officer to expound on his or her theories. Utilize the formulas described before, and proceed in a step-by-step manner, depicting how the conclusion or conclusions were reached.

Example: Using the same situation as before, it was found that the subject had a BAC of .14%, four hours after the accident. Determine the number of Ounces present at .14%. The person's body weight should be obtained at the time of the arrest. If they cannot or will not tell you, look at their driver's license, or if all else fails, estimate. For the sake of this example, the person's weight is 180 pounds.

Step One: Determine the number of ounces of Alcohol at .14% BAC.

$$OzETOH = \frac{BAC}{.10} \times 2 \times \frac{BW}{150}$$

$$OzETOH = \frac{.14}{.10} \times 2 \times \frac{180}{150}$$

$$OzETOH = 1.4 \times 2 \times 1.2$$

$$OzETOH = 3.36$$

Step Two: Add to 3.36 ounces, the amount eliminated during the 4 hours after the accident occurred.

1/3 of an Ounce has been eliminated each hour after peaking, or .33 Oz. X 4 = 1.33 Oz.

It has now been determined that there were 4.69 ounces present in the subject's body at the time the accident occurred. By factoring this amount of ETOH into formula (1), it is found that the person had the following BAC at the time of the accident.

Step Three: Determine the BAC at the time of the accident.

$$BAC = \frac{OzETOH \times .05 \times 150}{BW}$$

$$BAC = \frac{4.69 \times .05 \times 150}{180}$$

$$BAC = 4.69 \times .05 \times .834$$

$$BAC = .20\%$$

Intoxication

"**Intoxication**" is the term given to describe the outward manifestations of an impaired Central Nervous System. It refers to the reduction, or loss, of normal human physical and mental faculties, and is based upon measurable changes in an individual's performance of a specific task. Within the context of this manual, the task is the operation of a motor vehicle.

The term "**drunk**," on the other hand, is a generalizing word, denoting a particular type of observed behavior, which has nothing to do with impairment of a person's ability to operate a motor vehicle. Intoxication refers to: "**impairment of the ability to operate a motor vehicle.**"

Impairment

"**Impairment**" refers to the injury or disease to the Central Nervous System and, by association, the ancillary structures. At low-level concentrations, the drug fosters a psuedo-stimulant effect. This is a false perception, caused in part by a release from the inhibitory control of the cerebral cortex. In fact, the first mental processes affected are those that depend on the cerebral cortex control. Remember, this area of the brain is the first to be effected. It regulates the center of higher mental activity and the component function known as Judgment.

Judgment

"**Judgment**" is a term given to various decision-making aspects of human behavior such as:

- Social Inhibitions
- Euphoria
- Perception of Reality
- Risk Assessment
- Self-Evaluation

1. **Social Inhibitions** – Depression of learned social and cultural inhibitions results in:

    - An individual demonstrating inappropriate behavior that would ordinarily be hidden, due to social prohibition of certain types of conduct.

    b) The release of suppressed hostility which, though not necessarily caused by the Police Officer's presence, is nevertheless, often directed toward the Officer.

Officer Safety Issue

2. **Self Evaluation** – Is the ability of an individual to judge his or her own behavior or performance in a particular situation or testing process.

    a) Individuals, when required to perform a specific task, both in an alcohol-free state and when intoxicated, evaluate themselves as performing better with alcohol than when alcohol-free. Independent observations, however, clearly reveal that when intoxicated, they perform the task slower and with more errors. An intoxicated person very simply loses the ability to judge his or her own performance. This leads to driving behaviors which would never be observed when the individual is alcohol-free.

3. **Risk Assessment** – Is the ability to determine what risks are acceptable and to understand the consequences of behaviors. An intoxicated person may accept risks, which would be unacceptable when sober.

4. **Euphoria** – Ethyl Alcohol also has the ability to create a feeling of well-being. The "warm fuzzies," if you will.

5. **Perception of Reality** – Because of an artificial feeling, a person's perception of reality is altered. He or she does not perceive the hazards inherent in the driving process. Therefore, as an example, he or she may feel comfortable traveling faster than safe and prudent in a residential area.

As consumption continues and the alcohol concentration level increases, memory, concentration and finer discrimination abilities are progressively diminished. Further elevation of the Ethanol level causes obvious emotional instability, loss of sensory-motor coordination, and the inability to walk and stand. Eventually, it precipitates anesthesia and, ultimately, death.

It is difficult to place numeric values to specific impaired characteristics. Factors relating to the purity and potency of the drug or drugs, dissimilar mental and physical characteristics inherent in all human beings such as, weight, age, and concurrent drug usage will cause differing levels of toxicity. The information found in Figure 8, prepared by the National Highway Safety Transportation Safety Administration, can help one better understand the relationship between BAC and manifestations of intoxication.

There is a much lower standard of evidence for "intoxication with regards to the operation of a motor vehicle" than there is for the common pedestrian "drunk". The "drunk" is considered impaired when there are obvious visible indications of inebriation, and can be in violation of the law if they are a danger to themselves or others. The driver of a motor vehicle is considered intoxicated when subtle functions of the CNS are affected causing a lack or diminishment of judgment.

Because of the various aspects of alcohol tolerance, judging an individual's level of intoxication can be very difficult when based solely on visual observations. Interpersonal relationships and social position often influence one person's judgment of another's' intoxication. The best method of determining intoxication, and hence impairment, is by accurate, scientific field testing.

.05% to .08%	Majority of individuals demonstrate some level of mental and physical impairment. Behavioral changes might occur. Judgment is definitely impaired. Fine muscular coordination is impaired and complex reaction time is lengthened.
.08% and above	All persons intoxicated with regards to the operation of a motor vehicle.
.30% and above	Severe Intoxication

Figure 8: NHTSA table of BAC levels and behaviors with regards to motor vehicle operation.

Physical Characteristics of Intoxication

Hearing

Although there is no known effect on the physical mechanism of hearing, alcohol does seem to raise the minimal level of noise at which a person will respond. The investigator may observe an intoxicated person raising their voice to compensate for this perceived hearing loss.

Smell

The nasal nerves are sensitive to even small quantities of alcohol. It will very quickly dull the sense of smell, and the drinker will be unaware of even his or her own odor.

Taste

Alcohol also dulls the taste sensation, resulting in most foods tasting bland.

Vasodilation

Alcohol causes a relaxation of venous and arterial walls, which results in more blood profusing the peripheral areas of the body. This is responsible for the flushed face observed in certain individuals who have consumed moderate to high amounts of alcohol. It also leads to additional heat loss from the body, because of the increased blood flow near the outer surfaces.

Cognitive Thought Processes

Intoxication causes memory loss, loss of cognitive thought processes and, at low BAC levels, impaired judgment. Overall, the intoxicated individual is not able to function appropriately. It leads to a shortened attention span and the inability to concentrate on specific tasks, such as Field Sobriety Tests.

Malnutrition

Malnutrition can result because while alcohol contains enormous amounts of calories, it has no nutrients. Cirrhosis of the liver, gastritis and lowered resistance to disease are common adverse affects to the continuous consumption of Ethanol.

Muscular Coordination

The human musculature is affected due to the depression of nerve transmissions to the muscles. At low BAC levels, fine muscular coordination is affected, but as the levels increase, large muscle groups become impaired, ultimately causing gross muscular incoordination. If the BAC continues to rise, involuntary muscles become completely impaired and respiration ceases, resulting in death. Because of this effect on the muscles, reaction time is lengthened. In fact, research has shown that above .08% BAC, reaction time is lengthened by 3 to 4 times.

Vision

Visual Blurring - Alcohol causes a blurring of vision, because it depresses the coordination between the eyes so they do not focus equally on the same spot as in normal vision. Though static visual acuity is generally unaffected, dynamic visual acuity (looking at moving objects) is impaired at BAC levels as low as .02%.

Diplopia – As alcohol concentrations increase, diplopia (double vision) occurs.

Visual Perception - Glare recovery time is increased. Peripheral vision narrows, making it more difficult to see hazards approaching from the sides. Peripheral vision is reduced by 10% at 160.8 ounces corresponds to 13.4, 12-ounce cans of beer. .05% BAC, and 28% at .10% BAC. Dim lights are more difficult to perceive and colors are harder to distinguish. It is not uncommon for an impaired person to drive their vehicle with the high beams operating. This is because they have a difficult time seeing. All of these **"loss of visual perception"** functions result in intoxicated persons overestimating distances and underestimating speed.

[Officer Safety Issue]

Fixation - A person may demonstrate the effect known as **"fixation,"** whereby an individual's vision becomes fixed on flashing lights. Because of this, it is not uncommon for an intoxicated person to drive into the back of police vehicles, which have emergency lights operating.

Positional Alcohol Nystagmus - This occurs when an individual lies down after consuming a large amount of Ethyl Alcohol. High concentrations of alcohol cause involuntary eye movements, which manifest themselves in the **"spins."** P.A.N. can result in severe disorientation, nausea and vomiting.

Tolerance

Tolerance is usually defined as the effect resulting from the chronic use of a drug, necessitating larger doses to achieve a desired effect. Although this definition is certainly valid, it is important to note that a reverse of this concept is more informative when speaking of alcohol or other depressant drug tolerance. That is to say, consider tolerance as the circumstance wherein the expected behaviors are not observed.

With this reversal of definition in mind, two types of Tolerance can be explained in relation to alcohol impairment: Natural and Learned.

Natural Tolerance

Natural Tolerance can be defined in three distinct ways:
- Inborn
- Stress
- Physical
    - **Inborn**
        Individuals who have natural inborn tolerance to low levels of alcohol are able to perform a specific task as

well as, a sober person. As mentioned previously, this effect may result from the alcohol or drug lowering the individual's inhibitions in a testing situation. This type of tolerance has only been demonstrated at levels below .08%, and is most prominent between .04% and .06% BAC.

- **Stress**

In high stress or anxiety situations, adrenaline is released into the human body to stimulate the body's response to the source of stress. With respect to intoxicated individuals, this can result in the person appearing less intoxicated than they really are. Stress tolerance is only a temporary effect, lasting for a few minutes. Due to the transient nature of this response, it has been difficult to determine whether this effect results in a lessening of the influence of the alcohol, or if the adrenaline assists in making the individual more aware and able to consciously disguise their intoxication. For example, an intoxicated driver may be able to step out of the car and stand relatively correct for a few moments, but will ultimately lapse back into their obvious instability when the effects of the adrenaline wear off.

- **Physical**

The visible effects of a given alcohol concentration will always be greater in a person who is ill, as compared to the same person when healthy. Their normal physical and mental faculties are weakened by their illness, which increases the effects of alcohol.

An individual may consciously or unconsciously attempt to disguise their intoxication; nevertheless, they cannot alter the fact that their judgment, reactions and coordination are impaired. Stress tolerance will be less of a factor in a person who is ill or physically frail.

Learned Tolerance

Learned Tolerance can also be defined in three different ways:
- Behavioral
- Acquired
- Acute

- **Behavioral**

    This is the result of an environmental influence, such as social setting, personality, mental state and the social customs associated with alcohol consumption. An individual will behave differently in dissimilar social settings even though the alcohol concentration in that person is the same. An individual's mood or sense of well-being can also influence behavior in different settings. For example, if a person is depressed and unhappy, consumption of alcohol or other drugs will force them into an even more depressed and unhappy state of mind. This effect is usually best observed at low levels of an alcohol concentration, because higher levels will alter the person's perception of reality, and it doesn't matter what their emotional level was in the first place.

- **Acquired**

This is the result of the chronic use of alcohol or drugs. A chronic user of alcohol is accustomed to the effects of the drug, and may attempt to compensate for these effects. These persons attempt to alter their behavior in order to lessen the outward manifestations of intoxication. Tests demonstrate that these persons are indeed impaired in judgment, reaction and coordination, but have learned through experience to disguise their outward appearance.

- **Acute or "Mallenby Effect"**

The Acute Effect, also known as the "The Mallenby Effect," is the result of an individual comparing their own assessment of their present condition with that of their past condition of intoxication.

During the absorption phase of alcohol consumption, the individual compares his or her perceived state with their condition when alcohol free. As an example, a person who has acquired an alcohol level of .15% compares their condition to that when alcohol-free. Their perception has been altered to the extent that the effects of the alcohol are over estimated. In other words, the person feels extremely intoxicated.

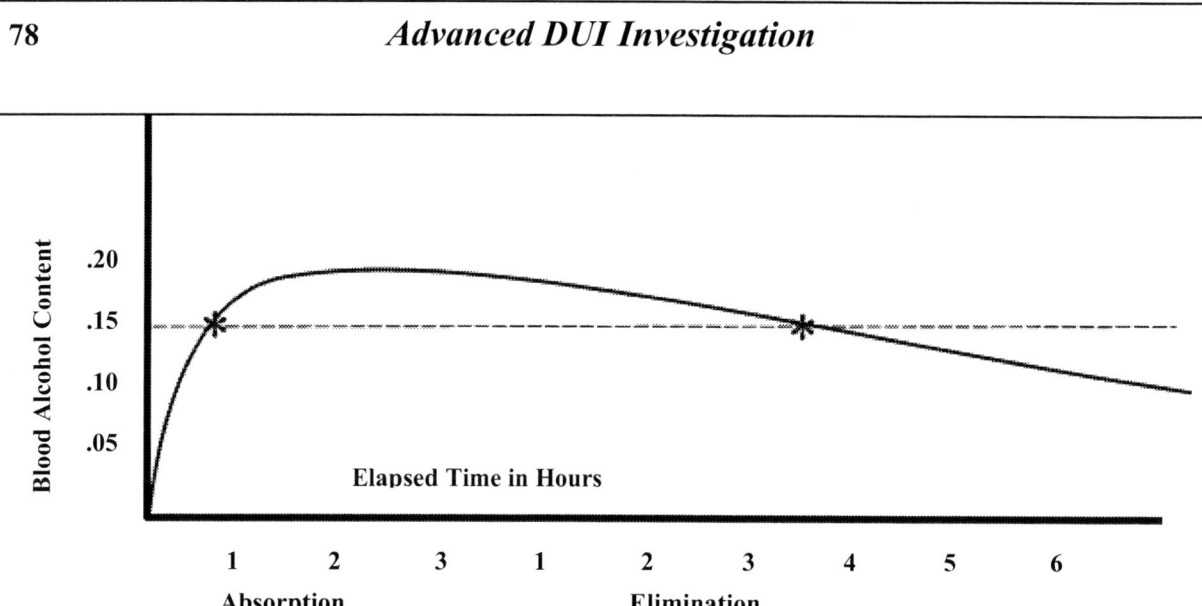

Figure 9: Acute or Mallenby Effect

Later, after the alcohol concentration has peaked and he or she enters the elimination phase, they again compare their condition with how they perceived themselves during the absorption phase. For example, after four and one-half hours in the elimination phase, they again compare their state of impairment with that when they were at the peak level. Their perception has been altered to the extent that the effects of their present state of intoxication are underestimated. They do not feel as if they are as intoxicated as when they had previously perceived their impaired state.

Elimination

Alcohol and other exogenous drugs are eliminated from the human body in the following manners:

1. Metabolism
2. Excretion

3. Evaporation
4. Breathing Process

Metabolism

Metabolism is the process whereby food is broken down into waste matter. It accounts for the elimination of most of the alcohol consumed. As the alcohol passes again and again through the liver, it is processed with the enzyme Alcohol Dehydrogenase (ADH). The alcohol is oxidized into simpler compounds, such as acetaldehyde and acetic acid. The acetaldehyde and acetic acid are then broken down by another process into carbon dioxide and water.

Excretion

A small percentage of the Ethyl Alcohol is excreted, unchanged, through the bladder and into the urine. The amount of Ethanol in the urine is proportional, within certain limits, to the Ethanol concentration of the blood.

Evaporation

Alcohol is also dissolved in the body's perspiration, transported through the skin and evaporated into the surrounding air.

Breathing Process

Some of the ingested alcohol is also exchanged into the lungs and exhaled from the body in the breath. This exchange of alcohol from the blood to the breath occurs in the alveoli of the lungs,

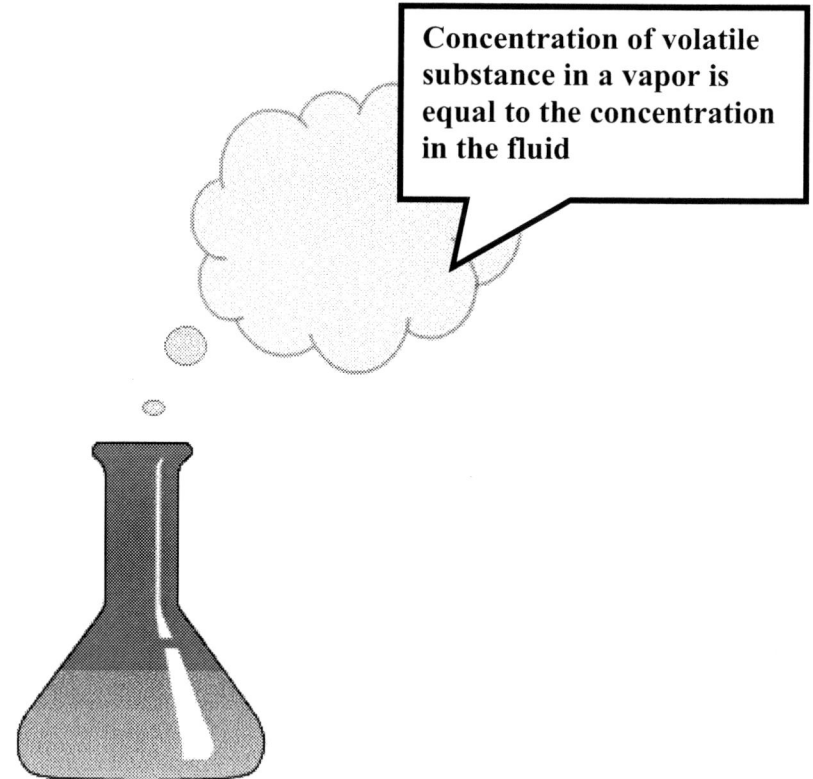

Figure 10: Depiction of Henry's Law

which are minute sacs richly supplied with blood from the heart. The separation between the alveoli and the blood capillaries is permeable to certain vapors, and is where the exchange between oxygen and carbon dioxide takes place. By diffusion, a portion of the alcohol, in the same ratio as the blood, enters the lungs and is transferred from the capillaries to the alveoli, and eventually moved through the respiratory system out of the body.

Henry's Law (See Figure 10) can best explain the exchange of alcohol from the blood to the breath. It demonstrates that the concentration of a volatile vapor in the air above a fluid is proportional to the concentration of the volatile substance in the fluid. This allows for the use of breath analysis machines.

As stated before, body weight affects the Alcohol concentration when a given amount of alcoholic beverage is consumed. Assume that a normal healthy person, having a body weight of 150 pounds, consumes enough Ethanol to produce an alcohol concentration of .015% in the blood. The person does not have another drink for an hour. Now recall that the body is capable of eliminating alcohol at a rate of .015% per hour. The rate of absorption equals the rate of elimination. At the end of approximately one-hour, there will be no alcohol remaining in the body.

In order to accumulate alcohol in the body, the rate of absorption must exceed the rate of elimination. When absorption has been completed, consumption ceases and the alcohol concentration gradually begins to fall as the alcohol is eliminated. Overall, there are three phases involved in the consumption of alcohol: Absorption, Peak and Elimination Phases.

There are three functions which take place within each phase: Absorption, Distribution and Elimination. The slope of each phase will vary according to the various factors affecting the functions. In order to determine whether a person's alcohol concentration is rising, peaking or falling depends on which phase, and the function within any phase they are in, at any given time. If the rate of elimination is greater than the rate of absorption, then the net result is a lowering of the alcohol concentration. In actuality, all three functions generally occur at the same time, until the consumer completely stops drinking Ethyl Alcohol.

The best method of determining the alcohol concentration in a human body, at any particular time, is to conduct an analysis of a suitable specimen of blood, breath or urine. When a chemical test is administered, the results demonstrate the alcohol concentration at the time the sample was collected. The test cannot determine whether the subject was in the absorption, peak or elimination phase.

> **Regardless of the method, elimination is a physiological process and is not significantly effected by exercise or stimulants such as coffee. Neither stimulants nor exercise will affect the results of a breath, blood or urine alcohol test. Currently, the only proven way to sober is to allow sufficient time for the body to eliminate the alcohol.**

SECTION FOUR: Depressant and Stimulant Drugs . . . And Others

DEPRESSANTS

Symptomatically, Alcohol and Depressant intoxication mimic each other. For this reason, depressants have been referred to as "solid alcohol," and alcohol as "liquid depressant." The consumption of alcohol and depressant drugs affects those areas of the brain that control the learned conscious and voluntary actions of the Cerebral Cortex. For example, a dosage of alcohol and/or depressant drug may initially manifest itself by reducing social inhibitions and the ability to perform complex tasks that require concentration and fine muscle control. A small dosage can significantly affect a person's ability to drive a vehicle. The consumer's motor skills, reflexes and judgment are impaired, even at low levels of intoxication.

With the administration of larger dosages, a condition that is comparable to obvious drunkenness is experienced by the consumer and manifests as observable symptoms of intoxication. They first affect those areas of the brain that control a person's conscious, voluntary actions. They are once again compared to alcohol, in that they reduce social inhibitions, impair the ability to divide one's attention, slow reflexes, impair judgment and impair vision and coordination. When a high enough dose of alcohol or a depressant is consumed, the user's autonomic motor control center may become so completely suppressed that the cardio-pulmonary control center (Medulla Oblongata) ceases to function, and death results from suffocation.

Automatism

A significant danger with depressants is the potential for automatism. Automatism is the phenomenon where the consumer takes a dosage, forgets that they have taken it, then takes another, compounding the effects.

Potentiation & Synergism

Depressants can also have the effects of potentiation and synergism. This is the effect of a combination of two or more depressants that is greater than their proportionate amount.

Although alcohol and drugs have the capability of depressing autonomic function, depressant drugs pose the greater hazard of causing death. The consumer will usually pass out or vomit before enough alcohol has been ingested to cause respiratory or cardiac distress. On the other hand, it is very easy to consume enough depressant drug to cause death.

In addition to Ethyl Alcohol, the depressant category includes;
- Analgesics – which relieve pain
- Tranquilizers and Sedatives – which produce relief from anxiety and sleeplessness
- And
- General Anesthetics – which produce loss of sensation and unconsciousness.

Analgesics

Very simply, analgesics are drugs that relieve pain. Physical pain is part of a larger sensation called the "pain experience," which includes, in addition to the sensation of pain, all the associated emotional sensations experienced by a particular person under

Impairing Drugs

specific circumstances. For this reason, there is a wide variation in individual response to the sensation of pain. Over-the-counter analgesics, such as aspirin, acetaminophen and ibuprofen, do not have chemical properties that cause impairment of the type this course is concerned about. When analgesics are mentioned, therefore, it will pertain only to the types which have "impairing" or "mind-altering" characteristics.

Analgesics act in three ways to affect the human body;
1. By elevating the pain threshold;
2. By altering the attitude or mood of the person, from one of concern to one of detachment, thus promoting a sense of well-being or mild euphoria; and
3. By producing a sedative effect and drowsiness.

Narcotic Analgesics (Opioids)

Opium is one of the oldest pain relievers on record. Its active ingredients are the alkaloids: Morphine, Codeine and Papaverine. Morphine and Codeine belong to the Phenanthrene group, while Paparvine is known as a Benzylisoquinoline derivative. Morphine and Codeine act mainly on the Central Nervous System, whereas Paparvine acts on the smooth muscle groups of the human body.

Opiates elicit their effects by activating opiate receptors, which are widely distributed throughout the brain and body. Once an opiate reaches the brain, it quickly activates the opiate receptors and produces an effect that correlates with the brain area involved. In other words, when the opiate receptors, in the area of the brain which controls speech, are activated, the individual's speech begins to be affected. Two important effects are produced by opiates; pleasure (reward) and pain relief. The brain itself also produces substances known as endorphins that activate the opiate receptors.

Within the reward system, the morphine activates receptors in the Ventral Tegmental Area, the Nucleus Accumbens and Cerebral Cortex. Research suggests that stimulation of the opiate receptors by morphine will result in feelings of reward, activate the pleasure circuit by causing greater levels of dopamine to be released within the Nucleus Accumbens. This causes an intense euphoria, or "rush," that lasts only briefly, and is followed by a few hours of a relaxed, contented state. This excessive release of dopamine and stimulation of the reward system is a leading component of addiction.

Synthetic Narcotic Analgesics

The search for analgesics which do not have the side effects of organic Narcotics led to the development of such drugs as: Demerol, Methadone, Anileridne, etc. Though they do lessen some side effects of the Narcotic category, they still cause a definite overall CNS depression and, consequently, a significant lessening of the mental and physical faculties necessary to operate a motor vehicle.

Impairing Drugs

The following compounds are found on the street as ingredients in the most commonly abused Narcotic and Synthetic Narcotic Analgesics:
- Morphine Sulfate
- Codeine (Tylenol w/Codeine, Empirin w/codeine, Robitussin A-C, Fiorinal w/Codeine, APAP w/Codeine)
- OxyContin (Oxycodone, Percodan, Percocet, Tylox, Roxicet, Roxicodone, Roxanol)
- Hydrocodone (Vicodin, Hycodan, Lorcet, Lortab, Tussionex)
- Hydromorphone (Dilaudid)
- Meperidine (Demerol)
- Diphenoxylate (Lomotil)
- Methadone
- Fentanyl
- Thebaine

Barbiturates

Barbiturates were first produced at the turn of the century, and used as an aid in the treatment of sleeping disorders and to relieve symptoms of diseases, such as Epilepsy, Parkinson's Disease, etc. They act at all levels of the CNS, especially the motor cortex, with the most noticeable impairing characteristics as mild sedation to deep anesthesia.

The following is a list of those Barbiturates found commonly on the streets:
- Secobarbital (Seconal)
- Amobarbital (Amytal)
- Pentobarbital (Nembutal)
- Phenobarbital (Luminal)

- Meprobamate (Miltown)
- Methaqualone (Quaalude)
- Tuinal

Muscle Relaxants

A sub-category of Barbiturates, with the same effects as other depressants is Muscle Relaxants. These drugs do not act directly on the muscle; rather, they act centrally in the brain and are more of a total body relaxant. The type most often found in conjunction with DUI investigations are those known as "centrally-acting skeletal muscle relaxants." Their consumption causes symptoms similar to mild doses of Narcotic analgesics, such as, drowsiness, dizziness, blurred vision, lightheadedness, low mental abilities, and impaired judgment.

The following is a list of those Muscle Relaxants commonly found on the street:
- Carispodal (Rela, Soma)
- Chlorzoxazone (Paraflex)
- Methocarbamol (Robaxin)
- Metaxalone (Skelaxin)

Tranquilizers

Tranquilizers, or Benzodiazepines, are a category of depressant covering a vast variety of chemical compounds capable of lessening anxiety and producing sleep. They are one of the most widely prescribed and abused drugs in the United States. Since their introduction, over 100 million prescriptions have been written each year, creating an enormous hazard to the safe operation of motor vehicles. Their purpose includes, but is not limited to, lowering of anxiety and muscle tension associated with psycho-motor agitation or "stress." Negative effects of the drugs are drowsiness, diminished muscular coordination and dizziness, reduced inhibition, diminished judgment, and poor cognitive skills.

The following is a list of tranquilizers, which are commonly found to be abused, or to be an important causative factor of impaired driving:

- Valium
- Tranxene
- Librium
- Xanax
- Ativan
- Versed

Heroin

Heroin is derived from opium poppy plant, and first produced in 1874 as a non-addictive alternative to morphine, which had enslaved thousands by its addictive characteristics. Unfortunately, Heroin soon proved to be more addictive than morphine, and because of the number of side effects, it became a controlled substance under a series of Congressional Acts in 1920. Although various opiates (codeine, morphine, dilaudid, etc.) are used in medical applications today, Heroin is not approved for any recognized medical use in the United States.

In general there are two forms of Heroin found in the United States. One is the brown powder form known as "Mexican

Brown." This form is usually found to be 2% to 5% pure. The common method of packaging the powder form of this drug is by "balloon." A quarter-gram of the chemical is enclosed in a balloon, which has been closed off and folded over into a ball. In this manner, the suspect can hide the package in his or her mouth and swallow it, if necessary, should a police officer approach. Because of the rubber balloon's consistency, it will withstand the body's acid, pass through the digestive track and, ultimately, retrieved later when excreted through the alimentary canal. A white powder form, with the same basic properties as Mexican Brown, known as "China White," is also available.

The second form, which has surpassed powder in usage, is "Tar Heroin." This form has been left in a brown, solid form. It is hard and chunky, but will turn soft and sticky when heated. Because Tar Heroin is not susceptible to being "stepped on" (because of its solid structure), it will be found in strengths varying from 40% to 80% pure. It is sold in very small amounts, (1/10 of a gram), obviously allowing it to be easily concealed.

When Heroin is introduced into the body, it is converted to morphine within two or three minutes. Before this conversion is completed, however, the Heroin enters the brain and produces a brief and intense feeling of euphoria, called a "rush." Thereafter, the drug produces an enormous depression of the Central Nervous System, accompanied by significant muscle relaxation. This intense relaxation results in the appearance of sleeping, or unconsciousness, known as "being on the nod." In fact, the consumer is conscious and fully aware of his or her surroundings.

Methadone

Methadone Hydrochloride is a synthetic opiate with a recognized medical use and a high potential psychological and physiological dependence. It is used as a sedative, cough reliever, painkiller and in the treatment of Heroin addicts.

German scientists developed Methadone during World War II, when their supply of natural opiate painkiller was cut off. Following the war, Methadone was approved for use in the United States. As a member of the synthetic Narcotic family, the symptomology of Methadone is identical to that of other opiates.

STIMULANTS

Stimulants are a class of drugs that enhance brain activity; that is, they cause an increase in alertness, attention and energy that are accompanied by increases in blood pressure, heart rate and respiration.

Historically, stimulants were used to treat asthma and other respiratory problems, obesity, neurological disorders and a variety of other ailments. As their potential for abuse and addiction became apparent, the use of stimulants began to wane. Now, stimulants are prescribed for treating a few health conditions, including narcolepsy, attention deficit hyperactivity disorder (ADHD), and depression that has not responded to other treatments. Stimulants may also be used for short-term treatment of obesity and asthma.

Stimulants, such as dextroamphetamine (Dexadrine) and methylphenidate (Ritalin), have chemical structures that are similar to key brain neurotransmitters called monoamines, which include norepinephrine and dopamine. Stimulants increase the levels of these chemicals in the brain and body. This increases blood pressure and heart rate, constricts blood vessels, increases blood glucose and opens the pathways of the respiratory system. In addition, the increase in dopamine is associated with a sense of euphoria that accompanies the use of these drugs which is of significance to DUI Investigators.

Stimulants cause users to feel an intense wave of physical and psychological exhilaration, which tends to keep them awake and alert. These drug types provide a significant mood elevation, but continued use forces depletion of the body's stored energy. This occurs when the drugs overtax the body and cause it to literally burn itself up. Vitamin and mineral deficiencies are common, due to inadequate nutrition, and as the user pushes himself or herself beyond what can be normally tolerated by the human body. Rapid and noticeable deterioration of health occurs. This is due to lowered resistance and disease. Prolonged use will cause damage to body organs, particularly the lungs, liver and kidneys. It also produces a heavy degree of psychological tolerance and a high degree of physical dependence. A psychotic state, characterized by chronic insomnia, anxiety, depression and fatigue can occur. Toxic psychosis, similar to paranoid schizophrenia and other delusional states, may result from either short or long-term use. Long-term psychosis may be permanent.

Not all users experience the same effects, nor will a person experience the same effects with each use. Repeated use and increased dosages create effects which range from extremely pleasant to terrifying as the use becomes more chronic and intensified. The acute positive effects of cocaine usually include a generalized state of euphoria, in combination with feelings of increased energy, confidence, and mental alertness. Many people feel more talkative, intensely involved in their interaction with others, more playful and spontaneous. Pre-existing shyness, tension and fatigue may instantly disappear.

With continued use, persons become progressively tolerant to the positive effects, while negative effects steadily increase. Rebound effects, such as dysphoria (disquietness, restlessness), and depressed behavior cause the individual to continually increase the dosage and frequency of use.

Stimulants are generally introduced into the body in one of three ways:
1. The hydrochloride, or salt form, is most commonly ingested by sniffing the substance into the nose, where it is absorbed through the mucous membranes of nasal passages. This is known as "snorting" or "tooting."

2. Cocaine hydrochloride is very soluble in water, allowing intravenous injection.
3. In the base form (known as Crack), cocaine is heated in a pipe, where it evaporates into fumes that are inhaled. The incredibly intense effects last for approximately 20 minutes.

Cocaine

Cocaine is a potent stimulant that is an alkaloid of the coca plant found primarily in South America. It has legitimate medical use as an anesthetic for ear, nose, eye and throat surgery. The illegitimate use of cocaine, however, has increased to incredibly high levels. It was once considered the drug of the rich, but an increased supply and demand and the introduction of "Crack" cocaine has caused the price to drop and, by correlation, enabled a wider use over all socio-economic levels.

People take cocaine mainly to alter their mood and mental state. The acute effects are all a direct result of cocaine-induced biochemical changes in brain activity. These produce desired changes in mood and consciousness but, as with all mood-altering drugs, the specific state of cocaine intoxication is difficult to describe. Both the quality and intensity of the cocaine-induced experience can vary markedly according to many different factors, including:

- The dosage
- The chronicity of use

- The method of administration the simultaneous use of other drugs
- The mood of the user
- The personality of the user
- The expectations and physical condition of the user
- The reason for taking the drug

and

- The setting and circumstances under which the drug is consumed.

Amphetamines

Chemically and physiologically, amphetamines are related to biologically-active chemicals known as Adrenaline and Epinephrine, which naturally occur within the human body. In the 1920s, during the search for drugs that would constrict blood vessels, amphetamines were synthesized for medical purposes. They were first used to treat colds, because they shrank the nasal membranes and gave temporary relief to stuffy nasal passages. Since then, more effective drugs with fewer side effects have been developed.

Today, amphetamines are medically prescribed for narcolepsy, depression and appetite control. It should be noted, however, that the *Handbook on Drug Dependence*, published by the American Medical Association, indicates that with the exception of hyperactivity in children, the use of stimulants is subject to varying degrees of controversy within the medical profession.

Drug abusers use amphetamines to push themselves beyond normal physiological limits. These individuals usually want to remain awake for long periods of time, with some degree of mental alertness, or to allegedly increase their physical capabilities. Others use them strictly for the euphoric high or intoxication.

There is also a danger of rapid deterioration of physical and psychological health, since amphetamines erase feelings of periods of time. This creates the same sort of stress to the body as any long period of exertion would create. The abuser does not allow his or her body to recuperate and permanent damage or death can result from the constant onslaught on the body systems.

> **As is true of alcoholic intoxication, the euphoric feeling produced by a stimulant drug can be extremely hazardous when combined with the driving experience. The driver loses the ability to make valid risk assessments and may take chances they would otherwise not take when sober.**

There are more than 31 amphetamine preparations being distributed by approximately fifteen pharmaceutical companies. The most common are the following:

- Dexedrine
- Dexamyl
- Benzedrine
- Biphetamine

Impairing Drugs

- Desoxyn
- Preludin
- Retalin

Large proportions of the lawfully manufactured pharmaceutical amphetamines are unlawfully distributed; however, the most common forms of illicitly distributed stimulants are those which are manufactured in clandestine labs found throughout the country. These labs vary from crude bathroom-types to the highly complex commercial-type laboratories.

There are two basic types of illicitly manufactured amphetamines:
1. Amphetamine Sulfate
2. Methamphetamine Hydrochloride

Amphetamine Sulfate is manufactured in powder form and sold as small double-scored white tablets known as "Cross Tops" or "Minibeans."

Methamphetamines

Methamphetamine Hydrochloride, often called the "poor man's cocaine," was formally the drug of choice for outlaw motorcycle gangs. It has street names such as:
- Meth
- Crystal
- and
- Crank

It is usually cooked and sold in powder form and administered by injection directly into a vein. Manufacture and possession is a violation of federal and local laws.

Its appearance ranges from medium to large crystals, exhibiting colors that are almost transparent with a light yellow cast or a translucent, milky or almost pure white.

This drug should be no more potent or addictive than regular stimulants, if the drug were to be ingested in the usual manner (i.e., orally, nasally or intravenously). The ingestion method of "crack" or "ice, however, is by inhalation of vapors directly into the lungs via smoking. Because of this method, the potency of the drug is considerably more intense because of the larger amount consumed, per unit of time, per ingestion. If one compares the surface area of the nasal passage mucous membranes to that of the interior volume of the lungs, it becomes clear that a considerably larger quantity of drug can be ingested more rapidly and in a greater volume by inhaling as opposed to snorting or injecting. The "high" from smoking "ice" endures from 12 to 24 hours. "Crack" intoxication will usually last for 20 minutes to an hour. After bodily assimilation and distribution, large doses may be excreted into the urine unchanged for up to 72 hours after consumption.

HALLUCINOGENS

Hallucinogens are similar to naturally-occurring neurotransmitters and displace and interfere with the function of these body chemicals. In turn, dysfunction at the synaptic junction level precipitates either an increase or decrease (depending on the drug ingested) of transmissions between cells. The result is an over-reaction or under-reaction by the brain, with distortion of modalities, such as hearing, sight and sound, etc. It is important to note however, that the exact method of action of hallucinogenic drugs is not well understood. For example, Lysergic Acid Diethylamide (LSD), if consumed, remains present in the brain for approximately one hour, while the hallucinogenic effects may last 8 to ten hours longer. The drug is broken down and eliminated by normal metabolic process. It is then excreted from the body. Nevertheless, it is apparent to physiologists that these enzymes necessary to metabolize LSD is not present within the human body and obviously do not take an active part in the metabolic process.

Lysergic Acid Diethylamide (LSD)

Lysergic Acid Diethylamide was discovered less than 50 years ago and although it has been the subject of an incredible amount of research, it took over 20 years for the drug to become illegal in the United States. Initially researchers were aware that LSD, like many other drugs, posed certain problems. At the same time, they felt that the benefits of the drug outweighed the hazards. As additional research was undertaken, even more potentially dangerous adverse effects became obvious from its use.

Medical experimentation began in 1949. It was believed the LSD could reduce a patient's defensiveness and allow psychotherapists and patients to gain greater insight into repressed memories. In 1952, LSD was tried as a treatment for alcoholism. It was also used in the treatment of terminally ill cancer patients. The depression and pain these individuals experienced were sometimes lessened for a significant period of time, or it was found that the patients were better able to deal with the anxiety involved. Over the course of these experiments, many psychological complications and disorders were encountered. They can be separated into four categories that most commonly occur:

1. The Flashback – An LSD experience or "trip" can reoccur without the immediate ingestion of the substance. The flashback can occur shortly after the completion of an LSD trip, or as long as two years from the last ingestion.

2. Terror – Another common side effect is the fear or panic experienced by the consumer when he or she is unable to cope with the vivid, surreal and often horrifying images brought on by the use of the drug. This panic is more often experienced by the novice LSD user as opposed to those individuals who have taken the drug frequently and are more familiar with its effects. Medical and law enforcement personnel often encounter individuals who are experiencing an LSD panic or "bummer."

3. Psychosis – Use of LSD can also cause an extended period of psychosis, which may occur after only a single exposure.

4. Superman Complex – Other types of complications arise when a user believes he or she has certain unusual powers. This creates a "superman complex" where users feel invulnerable to their environment. A number of accidental deaths have been reported where users, for example, tried

Officer Safety Issues

to stop a moving train or attempted to fly off a multistoried building.

One of the amazing properties of LSD is that a minute amount produces an extremely intense and very long-lasting effect. The predominance of mental symptoms led researchers to believe that LSD accumulates in the brain; however, a number of investigations employing LSD, dyed by radioactive material, revealed that this is not true. In fact, after intravenous injections of the radioactive LSD, the bulk of the chemical concentrated in the small intestines, liver and kidneys. The infinitesimal amount that did reach the brain had dissipated in 45 minutes to an hour and, as mentioned before, the hallucinogenic effects last for several hours thereafter.

Peyote/Mescaline

Mescaline is the chief alkaloid extracted from the peyote cactus, and it produces hallucinogenic effects similar to those produced by LSD. Like amphetamine, mescaline belongs to the Amine group, and its chemical structure distantly resembles that of norepinephrine. It is usually ingested in the form of a soluble powder.

> **The central effects of LSD are those which are most readily observable and which include the stimulation of the stimulation of electrical activity within the brain. This stimulation of the Reticular Formation results in heightened sensitivity to sensory stimuli received through the sense organs (eyes, ears, nose, etc.)**

Psilocybin — Psilocybin is a drug derived from Mexican mushrooms that produce hallucinogenic effects similar to those produced by mescaline, but of shorter duration.

Marijuana — Use of Marijuana for drug purposes is usually related to the ingestion of the dried plant. In this form, the plant is dried, crushed and appears on the street as a green or brownish leafy material suitable for smoking or oral ingestion (such as being baked in brownies).

Historically, the potency of dried marijuana varies from 4% to 5% THC (Tetrahydrocannabinol). This low THC content is the fodder for decriminalization effort. That is, marijuana is not harmful and does not cause long-term impairment. Recently, however, the THC content has been found to be as high as 27% and because of this increased potency, marijuana is now being investigated for potential addictive producing properties, long-term health problems and other previously unknown negative effects.

Hashish — Hashish is prepared from the resinous secretions of the flowering parts of the cannabis plant, which has been dried several times to increase its THC content (5% to 12%). It is found in a variety of forms and colors, ranging from light green to dark brown or black in color. It is commonly formed into a ball shape or cake and cookie thin sheets.

Hashish Oil — Hashish oil is produced by the repeated extraction of the resin through the use of alcohol and heat. The resulting product is a

Tetrahydrocannabinol

viscous brown liquid with the consistency of molasses, with a THC concentration ranging from 20% to 69%. A drop of the substance can equal the psychoactive strength of a typical marijuana cigarette. When smoked in cigarette form the body absorbs less than 50% of the total THC. The remainder is lost into the atmosphere in the escaping smoke. Once in the body, the effects of the THC is felt and exhibited within seconds of inhalation. These effects usually peak within 10 to 30 minutes and will continue for as long as 2 to 3 hours. When ingested orally, Hashish oil takes longer to show its effects, with the onset of action occurring in about an hour and peak effects within 4 to 5 hours.

The THC metabolizes into two other compounds, knows as:

11-Hydroxy-^-9-tetrahydrocannabinol (OH-THC)
and
11 Nor^-9-tetrahydrocannabinol (C-THC)

OH-THC and C-THC do not cause euphoric effects, but do cause visual, mental and motor impairment.

In addition to the lengthy plasma life of the marijuana metabolites, the THC attaches itself to the fatty tissues of the body, where it is stored and released at a much slower rate of dissipation than most other drugs. For the chronic user of Marijuana, this means that C-THC and OH-THC metabolites can be found in the urine up to 45 days from the last ingestion.

Because of the varying levels of THC and amounts of drug ingested, the effects of Marijuana will vary. It appears, however, that cannabis will interfere with a person's ability to pay attention to one or more stimulus simultaneously. This factor becomes crucial when attempting such tasks as driving a car. Because of this, "Divided Attention Testing" techniques can be very revealing.

Cannabis is being studied for potential medical applications; specifically, in the lowering of intra-ocular pressure for glaucoma patients, for asthma relief, for treating epilepsy and for relieving nausea induced by chemotherapy. Legal cannabis products include the brand names Marinol and Nabilone.

Inhalants

These types of chemicals are the drug of choice for the young. This is because of their availability and relatively low cost. The category consists of hydrocarbons, such as gasoline, glue, paint, paint thinners and products know as correction fluid.

The active ingredient in these substances is Toluene, a transparent hydrocarbon distilled from coal tar. When the vapors are breathed, they rapidly replace oxygen with hydrocarbon, which the human body finds extremely toxic. It causes a sense of semi-suffocation, which is manifested as a euphoric sense of well-being. The impairment caused by an inhalant is roughly the same as that of alcohol intoxication; however, the effects are very short-lived. Once the subject breathes fresh room air or bottled oxygen, the symptoms quickly fade. For this reason, Field Sobriety Tests must be conducted quickly, and careful documentation, by video and

Club Drugs

audio recording must be made, showing the extent of intoxication. Unless a blood sample is obtained immediately, there is slim chance of obtaining a chemical result. The substances wear off too quickly.

It is very difficult to classify these drugs into a single category. Their symptomology varies a great deal between those of the depressant, stimulant and hallucinatory categories. Research has shown that party drugs can produce a wide range of unwanted effects, including hallucinations, paranoia, amnesia, and, in some cases, death. When used with alcohol, these drugs can be even more harmful because they work on the same brain mechanisms as alcohol and, therefore, may produce a synergistic effect (see Polycombinations) by dangerously boosting the effects of both substances. As stated before, there are great differences among individuals and how they react to foreign chemicals, and no one can predict how he or she may respond to these substances.

The following drugs are the most common found on the streets and should be of significant concern to the DUI investigator:
- Ecstacy
- GHB
- Rohypnol
- Ketamine

Ecstacy

"X," "Adam," and "MDMA" are slang name for the drug Ecstacy. Its chemical name is: **Methylenedioxy-methamphetime**. It is a stimulant and a hallucinogen and ostensibly used to improve the consumer's moods or to boost their energy level. Research has shown that chronic abuse damages the brain's ability to think and regulate emotion, memory, sleep and pain.

GHB

This drug is known colloquially as "G," "Liquid Ecstacy," and "Georgia Home Boy." Its chemical name is **Gamma-hydroxybutrate.** GHB can be made in simple home labs by using recipes with common and easily found ingredients. At low doses, GHB can relax the user, but as the dose increases, the sedative effects result in sleep and eventual coma or death.

Rohypnol

"Roofie" or "Roche" is tasteless and odorless. It mixes easily in carbonated beverages. Rohypnol causes amnesia. Other effects include low blood pressure, drowsiness, dizziness and confusion.

Ketamine

This compound is an anesthetic known on the street as "Special K," or "K." Small doses of Ketamine result in the loss of attention span, learning ability and memory. High doses cause delirium, amnesia, high blood pressure, depression and severe breathing problems.

> **Drugs such as Ecstasy, GHB and Rohypnol are very popular among younger age groups. This prompts the absolute need for DUI investigators to be cognizant of their effects and the consequences of individuals operating motor vehicles while impaired by these substances.**

POLYCOMBINATIONS

In our society today, the incidence of alcohol consumption in combination with other types of drugs (illicit or prescribed) has become more and more commonplace. This type of usage will manifest itself in several forms:

- Significant observational impairment with low alcohol BAC's and subsequent test results indicating other Central Nervous System depressants.
- The presence of alcohol, but confusing outward manifestations of impairment and subsequent test results, indicating the presence of Central Nervous System stimulants.
- Very confused observable impairment cues, with test results indicating both depressant and stimulant drugs.

There can be as many combinations of different drugs as there exist in the modern pharmacopoeia; however, combining chemical agents will produce one of three types of reactions:

1. Additive
2. Synergistic
3. Antagonistic

Additive Effect

The additive effect is observed when a given dose of alcohol, as an example, and a given dose of another chemical agent produces the same effect as the two doses of the chemical or two doses of the alcohol.

Mathematical analogy for the additive effect is:

$$1 + 1 = 2$$

Synergistic Effect

The synergistic effect occurs when a combination of a dose of alcohol and a dose of a chemical agent forces an effect greater than the sum of their effects.

Mathematical analogy for the synergistic effect is

1 + 1 = 3 or higher

When two or more drugs, which have similar or identical pharmacological actions and effects, have been consumed together, they tend to enhance the observable outer manifestations of each other. For example, alcohol and Valium both produce depressant-type impairment. When taken in combination, however, the observable signs or cues of impairment become highly exaggerated.

Antagonistic

When two or more drugs which cause opposing pharmacological symptoms are taken in combination (depressant vs. stimulant or alcohol vs. cocaine), the actions and effects of the opposing symptoms may mask or minimize the effects of one or both of the consumed drugs.

An example often noted by investigating officers is that of an individual intoxicated by a depressant, alcohol for example, which is then counteracted by naturally-occurring adrenaline. When a person is stopped by a Police Officer, they normally experience fear. This fear forces the body to pump relatively large amounts of adrenaline, a stimulant, into the system and temporarily offsets the depressant value of the alcohol. It must be emphasized that this antagonism lasts only a few moments, until the impairing effects of the Ethyl Alcohol overcomes the less potent effects of the adrenaline.

Because of the acceptance of alcohol, both socially and legally, and the role it plays in social settings where other types of drug use might be anticipated, the combination of alcohol with other drugs occurs very frequently. It should be considered the most common of all forms of poly-combinations.

An attempt to predict the behavior of an individual who has consumed more than one type of drug is ultimately doomed to failure because of the following variables:
- Variability of intestinal absorption
- Competition for plasma
- Drug metabolism
- Action at the receptor sites
- Variability of renal excretion
- Electrolyte imbalances
- Types of drugs involved

Due to the dynamics of human physiology and the unpredictability of abused drugs, it is impossible to be absolutely sure what the observable behavior and effects of different combinations of drugs would ultimately be. For the DUI investigator, there are more significant considerations to be taken into account.

The standards for chemical actions and effects are based on probabilities of observable symptoms in a normal human being.

The Articulable and Recordable Indications of Driving Impairment

When evaluating a subject to determine driving impairment, however, three simple concepts regardless of either single or poly-drug use, must be kept in mind":

1. Articulable evidence of some sort of **DRIVING PATTERN,** indicating the possibility of an impaired driver.
2. Articulable evidence of **PHYSICAL DEMEANOR,** indicating impairment,
   and
3. Articulate the inability to perform "divided attention" **FIELD SOBRIETY TEST.**

Chapter Three: Investigative Process

Section One: Introduction

The Law Enforcement Code of Ethics states the following:

"As a Law Enforcement Officer, my fundamental duty is to serve mankind; to safeguard lives and property; to protect the innocent against deception; the weak against oppression or intimidation; and the peaceful against violence or disorder; and to respect the Constitutional rights of all men to liberty, equality and justice...."

In order to fulfill the obligations stated above in the Code of Ethics, Police Officers must actively participate in the detection, investigation and prosecution of DUI drivers. This is a difficult endeavor, given the lack of manpower and the overwhelming numbers of violators. It is a rather nasty task, due to the disdainful and repugnant nature of some intoxicated persons, nevertheless, it is these individuals who kill hundreds and maim and cripple thousands of people each year. Irrespective of the odious chore involved, it is imperative that Police Officers make a concerted and consistent effort to reduce the incredible hurt and anguish caused by the intoxicated driver.

Ideally, the prevention of this type of offense lies in the education and personal responsibility of each and every driver. The hope is held, that eventually everyone who drives a motor vehicle will do so alcohol and/or drug-free. The reality of the situation is however, that our society will never be free of those who force this incredible carnage upon our society. Legal sanctions in the form of DUI and DWI laws must be a close partner to driver's education and self-responsibility. Police Officers must be given the tools with which to detect, process, and ultimately lawfully arrest large numbers of violators. This takes training and experience. The effect is that of a societal pressure imposed upon those individuals so inclined to drive while under the influence of alcohol and/or drugs.

> **To accomplish the goal of deterring the DUI violator, Law Enforcement Officers must possess a thorough knowledge of the statutes within their own states governing this behavior.**

ELEMENTS OF THE OFFENSE

To establish "Probable Cause" for an arrest, the following elements of the offense must be satisfied:

- A person
- Operating or in physical control
- A vehicle
- While under the influence of alcohol, another drug or both.

Person

All criminal and traffic law is based on the premise that a human being or a "person" must commit an offense.

Vehicle

This is a simple concept to grasp. In the vast majority of all jurisdictions, a motor vehicle must be utilized, by the offender, in order for an offense to occur.

Operating or Physical Control

The difference between these two legal concepts is somewhat vague. "Operating" is defined as the actual driving or operation (the vehicle is in motion, being driven by the subject). On the other hand, "Physical Control" is defined as the physical ability to operate, control or have dominion over a vehicle (the vehicle is not in motion, but the driver has the physical ability or capacity to operate the vehicle, and the person has dominion over the vehicle).

Under the Influence

The person must be found:
- To be Under the Influence of Alcohol and/or Drug/s
- Intoxicated

  or
- Impaired

The simplest way to establish the elements of this offense is to observe, correctly interpret and document the following:
1. A driving pattern or actual physical control.
2. The subject's physical demeanor.
3. By conducting roadside, Psycho-Motor tests or as they are more commonly known, Field Sobriety Tests.

Do not be misled however. It is possible to successfully prosecute a case, even though one or more of the above components is absent. The prosecution will be much easier and cleaner if some degree of all three investigative components is present.

SECTION TWO: Driving Patterns

Research conducted by the National Highway Traffic Safety Administration has shown that the following driving cues (validated for night operation only) can indicate that a person may be operating a motor vehicle while impaired.

1. **60% Almost Striking an Object or Vehicle**

    The observed vehicle almost strikes a stationary object or another moving vehicle. This includes: passing abnormally close to a sign, wall, building or other object, and causing another vehicle to maneuver in order to avoid a collision.

    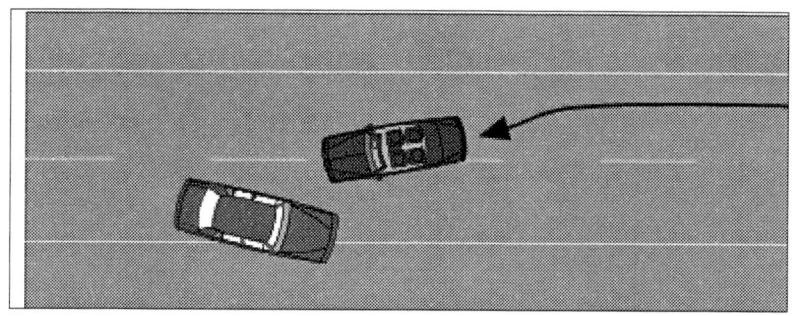

2. **65% Straddling Center or Lane Marker**

    The vehicle moves straight ahead with the lane marker between the left and right wheels.

    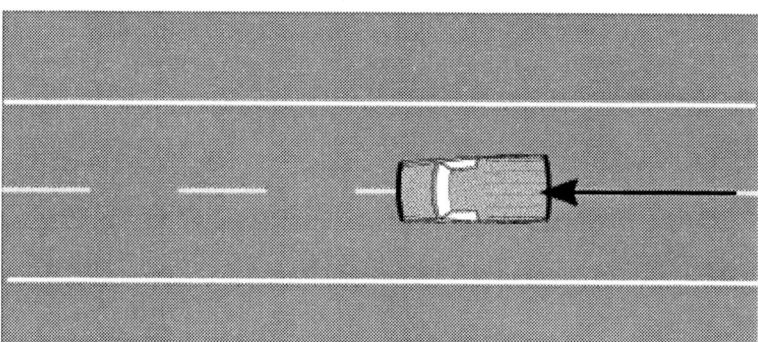

3. **50% Following Too Closely**

The vehicle is observed following another vehicle too closely. Failing to leave an appropriate amount of space ahead.

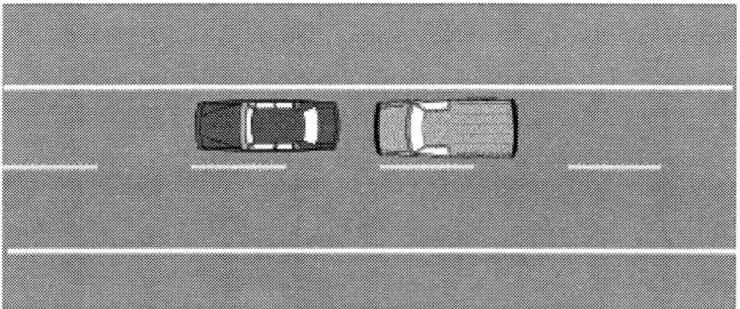

4. **30% Headlights Off**

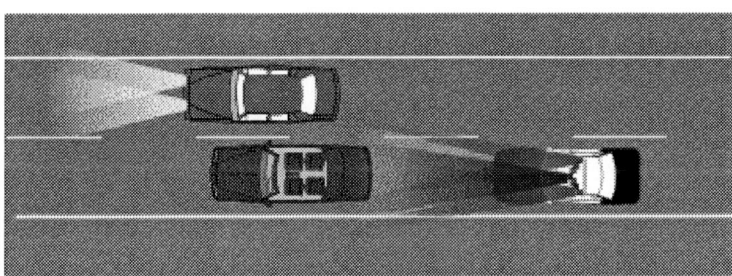

The observed vehicle is being driven with both headlights off, during a period of time, when the use of lights is required.

5. **45% Driving into Opposing or Crossing Traffic**

The vehicle is observed heading into opposing or crossing traffic under one or more of the following circumstances: driving the wrong way on a one-way street, or driving in an opposing lane.

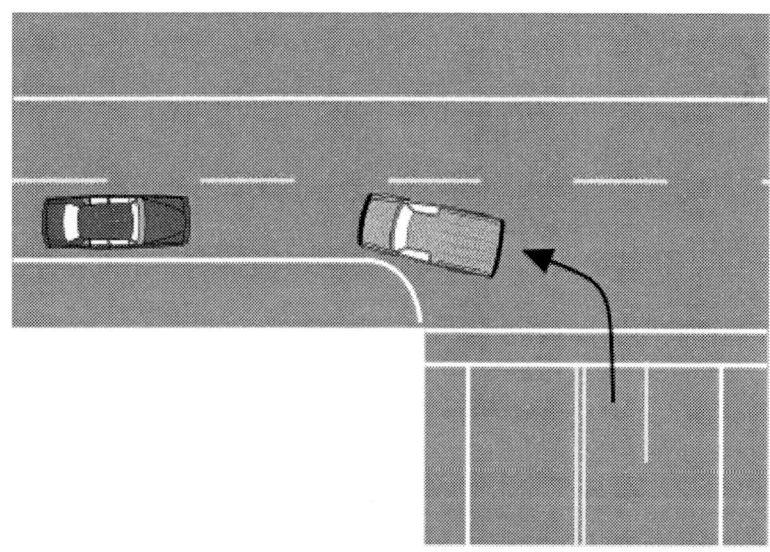

6. 45% Tires on Center or Lane Marker

The left hand set of tires, of the observed vehicle is consistently on the centerline, or either set of tires is consistently on the lane marker.

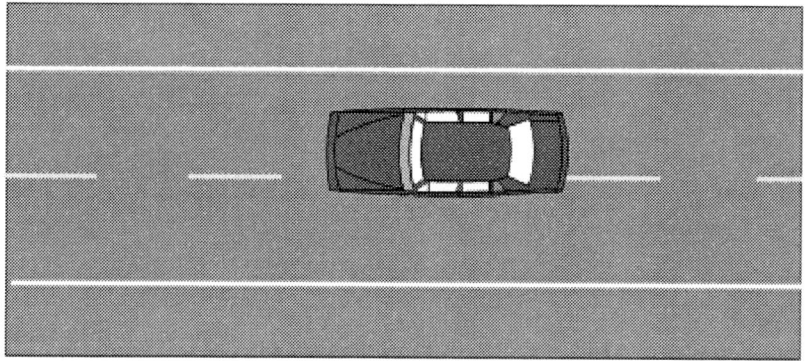

7. Turning with a Wide Radius

During a turn, the radius defined by the distance between the turning vehicle and the center of the turn is greater than normal.

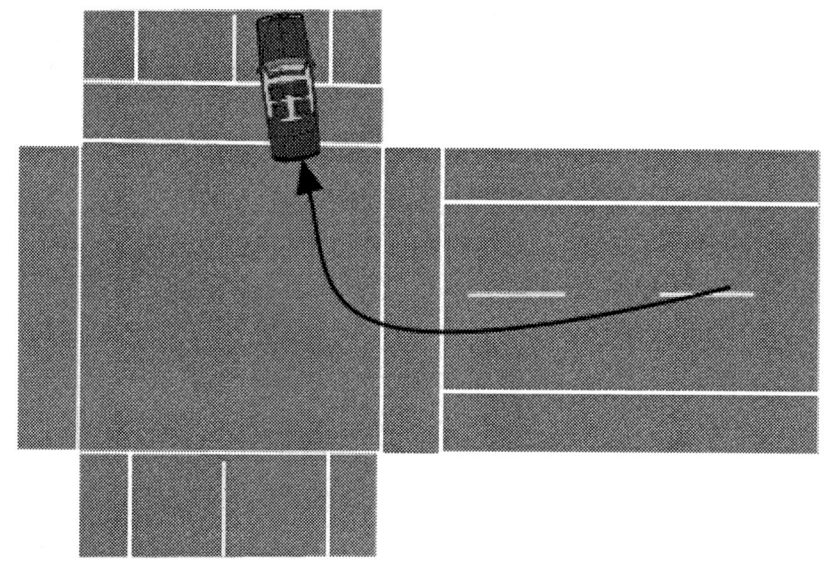

8. **30% Accelerating or Decelerating Rapidly**

   This cue encompasses any acceleration or deceleration that is significantly more rapid than that required by the traffic conditions. Rapid deceleration might be accompanied by breaking traction; rapid deceleration might be accompanied by a stop. The vehicle might alternately accelerate and decelerate rapidly.

9. **35% Stopping Inappropriately**

   The driver of the observed vehicle breaks unnecessarily, maintains pressure on the brake pedal, or brakes in an uneven or jerking manner.

10. **60% Weaving**

    Weaving occurs when the vehicle alternately moves toward one side of the roadway and then the other, creating a zigzag course. The pattern of a lateral movement is regular, as one steering correction is closely followed by another.

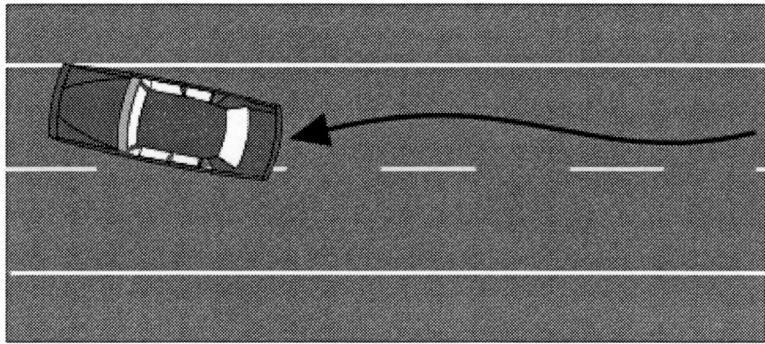

11. 60% Appears to Intoxicated

This cue is actually one or more of a set of indicators related to the personal behavior or appearance of the driver. Examples include:

- Eye Fixation
- Tightly gripping the steering wheel
- Slouching in the seat
- Gesturing erratically or obscenely
- Face close to the windshield
- Drinking in the vehicle
- Driver's head protruding from the vehicle.

12. 55% Driving on Other Than Designated Roadway

The vehicle is observed being driven on other than the roadway designated for traffic movement. Examples include:

- Driving at the edge of the roadway
- Driving on the shoulder, off the roadway entirely and straight
- Driving through turn-only lanes.

13. 45% Braking Erratically

The observed vehicle stops at an inappropriate location, or under inappropriate conditions. Examples include:

- Stopping in a prohibited zone
- For green traffic signals or for a flashing yellow traffic signals, unless necessary for right-of-way.

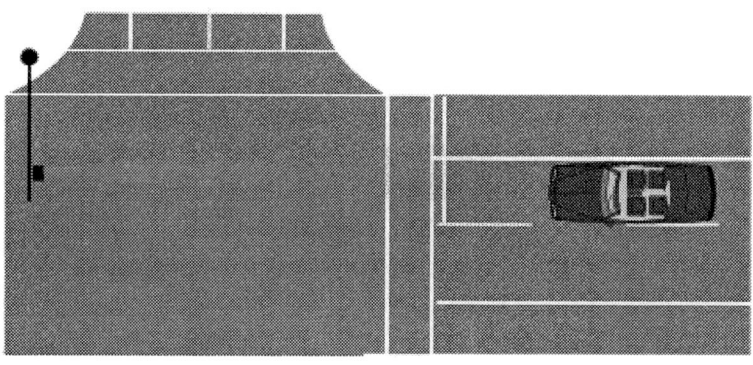

The critical element in this cue is that:

- There is no observable justification for the vehicle to stop in the traffic lane
- The stop is not caused by traffic conditions
- There are no traffic signals, emergency situations or related circumstances.

50% Drifting

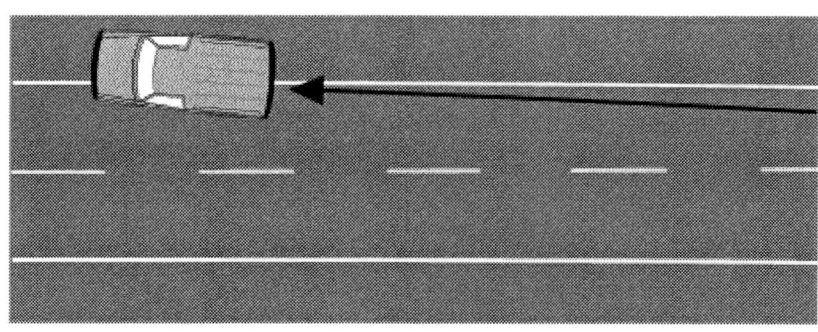

Drifting is a straight-line movement of the vehicle at a slight angle to the roadway. As the driver approaches a marker or boundary (lane marker, centerline, edge of a roadway), the direction of drift might change. Drifting might be observed within a single lane, across lanes, across the centerline or median, onto the shoulder or from lane to lane, etc.

15. **55% Swerving**

    A swerve is an abrupt turn away from a generally straight course. It might also occur directly after a period of drifting, when the driver discovers the approach of traffic in an oncoming lane, or discovers that the vehicle is going off the road.

    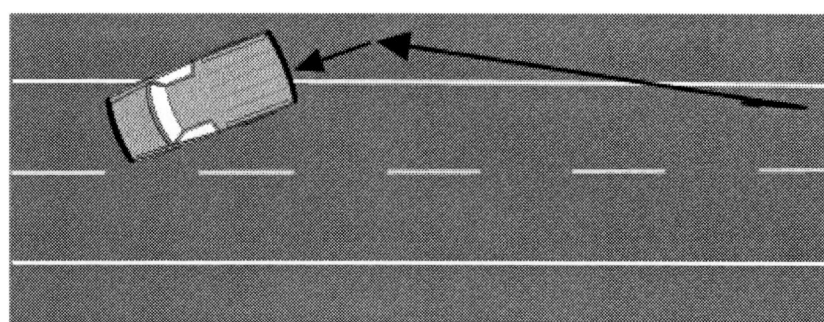

16. **40% Slow Response to Traffic Signal**

    The observed vehicle exhibits a longer than normal response to a change in traffic signals. For example, the driver remains stopped at the intersection for an abnormally long period of time after the traffic signal has turned green.

17. **50% Speed Slower than 10 MPH Below Limit**

    The observed vehicle is being driven at a speed more than 10 MPH below the limit.

18. 40% Signaling Inconsistent with Driving

This cue occurs when inconsistencies such as the following are observed:

- Failing to signal a turn or a lane change executed
- Signaling constantly with no accompanying driving action and
- Driving with hazard flashers operating.

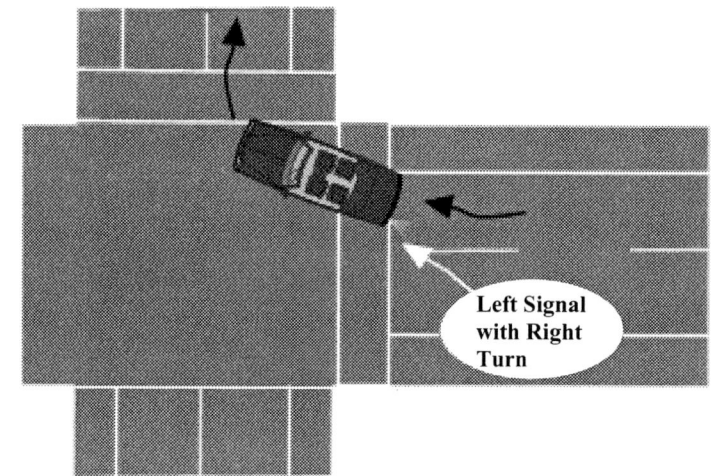

19. 35% Turning Abruptly or Illegally

The driver executes any turn that is abnormally abrupt or illegal. Specific examples include:

- Turning with excessive speed
- Turning sharply from the wrong lane
- Making an illegal U-turn
- Turning from outside a designated turn.

20. 50% Stopping Without Cause in a Traffic Lane

The critical element in this clue is that there is no observable justification for the vehicle to stop in the traffic lane.

Investigative Process

Traffic and Equipment Codes

A proficient knowledge of traffic and equipment codes is imperative. If an officer identifies a traffic or equipment violation, it is Probable Cause to believe that the driver has committed an offense and a traffic stop can be affected. From this point, further information may be developed, which may lead to Probable Cause to believe the driver was operating the motor vehicle while impaired by alcohol and/or drugs. In short, do not rely completely on the "classic" driving patterns to form an opinion of driving under the influence.

Traffic Accidents

This category requires some degree of additional expertise over and above the knowledge of DUI investigations. The ability to accurately investigate the causative factors of an accident is important for a Police Officer. In many instances, the causes of a collision are indicative of the impaired condition of the driver or drivers involved. Careful documentation of all evidence is absolutely necessary for any future adjudication of a DUI offense.

There will be occasions when an accident investigation shows that an intoxicated driver, involved in an accident, is not at fault. For example, the intoxicated driver is stopped in a line of traffic, waiting for a traffic signal to change and is rear-ended by another vehicle. This type of situation should be accurately documented. The fact that an individual was operating the vehicle, at the time of the accident, satisfies the necessity of establishing "driving" or "actual physical control," however, and a DUI investigation should be commenced. The tendency for an Officer to give this person a "break" must be resisted. It is unfortunate that he or she has been involved in an accident; nevertheless, they were operating or had physical control of a vehicle while impaired. Given other circumstances, the cause of the accident might have just as easily, rested on their shoulders. In fact, the chances of the individual being involved in a fatal accident are extremely high. In this case, the Officer would be investigating a vehicular homicide, rather than a misdemeanor DUI.

Witness Information

Obviously, when an Officer is notified of a witness report to a DUI situation, the Officer must attempt to locate the offender. Most witnesses who call into dispatch to report an intoxicated driver, however, will do so only on an anonymous basis. Indeed, there are public service announcements in the media informing citizens that they can anonymously report a "drunk driver." The courts have ruled that the anonymous report of an impaired driver by a citizen is not enough to stop a suspected violator with the intent of pursuing a DUI investigation. If a suspected DUI violator is located on the strength of an anonymous witness report however, the officer must attempt to develop his or her own driving pattern and thus, Probable Cause, to affect a stop. Even though a witness does identify himself or herself, the officer would be well-advised to solidify their decision to stop by cataloging and documenting a driving pattern or physical control.

SECTION THREE: Traffic Stop and Physical Demeanor

Traffic Stop

At the first indication of a DUI violation, documentation must begin. Video and audio recorders will replicate, in first person, the actions of the subject vehicle and the demeanor of the driver. This in turn supplies incontrovertible support for the decision to affect a DUI arrest.

In order to stop a vehicle for a suspected violation of a DUI offense, one or more of the following must be present:

1. Reasonable, articulable suspicion that the offense has or is taking place.
2. Probable cause that a moving traffic violation – "No matter how minor"- has taken place or is taking place.
3. Probable cause to believe that a vehicle equipment violation has taken place or is taking place.
4. An administrative traffic checkpoint, established under court guidelines, has produced reasonable, articulable suspicion or probable cause that the offense is taking place or has taken place.

In order to support these concepts, the following case law is offered:

Most state laws reflect the following statute, or one very similar, within their traffic codes: *"A motor vehicle may be stopped and the occupant detained by an enforcement officer when the enforcement officer has reasonable suspicion that criminal activity has occurred or is occurring."*

The Utah Supreme Court ruled in, State of Utah v. Gerard Cotero J. Lopez, the following: ***"...a police officer is constitutionally justified in stopping a vehicle if the stop is incident to a traffic violation committed in the officer's presence."*** It continues: ***"When an officer observes a traffic offense – however minor – he has probable cause to stop the driver of the vehicle."***

The same precedent added: "An observed violation, however, is not required. Stopping a vehicle may be justified when the officer has 'reasonable, articulable suspicion' that the driver is committing a traffic offense, such as driving under the influence of alcohol..."

Traffic stops on a DUI subject must be accomplished carefully. Close, well-documented scrutiny must be made of the subject vehicle as the driver brings it to a stop. Here again, a video camera is of incredible help.

After emergency lights are initiated, does the subject vehicle move slowly to the curb? Did it continue onward while the driver, consciously or unconsciously, disregarded the signal to stop? Or, did it pull over abruptly, strike the curb and bounce up onto the lawn of the adjacent property? Everything the vehicles does or doesn't do must eventually be placed into a report. The fairness and accuracy of this report will depend on the officer's abilities to report the occurrence in a swift and contemporaneous manner. A video record is, therefore, an error proof way of recording the facts so they can be precisely transcribed at a later time. A video recording of the driving pattern and the manner in which the vehicle came to a stop will most assuredly be presented later in a court of law. It will allow the officer to depict in first person why he or she felt that reasonable suspicion or probable cause was present to stop the vehicle in question.

Physical Demeanor

When the vehicle stops and as the investigating officer approaches, he or she must carefully observe and document the physical demeanor of the driver. Physical demeanor characteristics are those aspects of a person's appearance, actions or non-actions, speech, smells, etc., which give rise to the belief that he or she may be impaired. Note any and all characteristics that may be associated with those of an intoxicated person.

Investigators must learn to examine, understand and document all observable symptoms, no matter how slight, of driver impairment. In addition, it is imperative that DUI investigators know and be able to identify the underlying causes for the outer manifestations of intoxication. Remember that any observable symptom of impairment is an indication of an impaired Central Nervous System. Also, remember that a person can be impaired even though the subject driver presents no observable symptoms. For example, low-level alcohol content can severely affect judgment.

Cataloging and identifying indications of physical and mental driver impairment begin at the initial contact with the driver. This is during the period of time while the driver is still seated in the subject vehicle.

Severe Intoxication

First, look for the obvious signs. Does the subject appear to be "drunk?" Even an inexperienced officer will be able to detect the classic or obvious signs normally identified with those of a "drunk" person.

Examples:

1. Glazed and/or non-focusing eyes.
2. Mumbling or unintelligible speech.
3. Incoherence.
4. Difficulty in standing/walking, or inability to stand or walk.
5. Urination or defecation in clothing.
6. Inability to comprehend their native language or to follow simple instructions.
7. Heavy or strong smells of alcoholic beverage about the person and their breath.

Moderate Intoxication

The moderate intoxication cases will also be easy to identify and classify.

Examples:

1. Difficulty in following directions or instructions.
2. Divided attention impaired, as evidenced by initial questioning.
3. Smells of alcoholic beverages on the breath.
4. Difficulty in standing or walking or having to support themselves to any degree while out of the subject vehicle.

Low Level Intoxication

These types of cases may be difficult to identify and classify. It has been shown, however, that BAC levels as low as .04% to .05% can have a considerable effect on the cognitive thought processes

(judgment). An officer must not hesitate to process these types of offenses. Remember that all the factors listed below and any others observed by the investigating officer, must be documented. There may not be any obvious indications of intoxication, but specialized Field Sobriety Tests will show the extent of a person's impairment with regards to the operation of a vehicle. There will still be obvious signs of consumption of alcohol and/or drugs.
Examples:
1. Smell of alcoholic beverages on the breath.
2. Difficulty in performing tasks requiring fine motor skills, such as manipulating a driver's license from a wallet.

The National Highway Traffic Safety Administration (NHTSA) has developed valuable techniques for use by police officers in the investigation of DUI cases.

Divided Attention Questioning

In order to safely operate a motor vehicle, drivers must be able to accomplish a number of different tasks at the same time. Most of the tasks are a combination of both mental and physical tasks. The ability to perform these tasks is severely limited by the intake of alcohol and/or drugs; therefore, during the initial approach and contact with a driver, investigating officers should utilize *"Divided Attention Questioning"* techniques.

One of the ways in which alcohol and/or many drugs affect driving performance is to slow the processing of information within the Central Nervous System. This results in the impairment of the ability to perform multiple tasks. For example, the impaired driver may be able to steer in a straight line, but in doing so, utilizes all of his or her mental capability and disregards hazardous conditions occurring on the side of the roadway. The person may not notice a stop sign, a child playing or any other potential hazard that may present itself just ahead of their moving vehicle.

Divided Attention Questioning Techniques

After the traffic stop and initial contact with the driver, *"Pre-Exit Type"* questioning should be utilized. The purpose for this technique is to help identify and classify the degree of impairment and thus supports a request (or order) for the driver to step from the vehicle. These types of questions are divided into three categories:

1. Multiple requests
2. Rapid follow-up questions
3. Unusual questions

Multiple Requests

Start by asking the driver to produce a driver's license, registration and proof of insurance. This forces the driver to think about several mental and physical tasks at the same time. A driver, who is impaired even at a low level, will have difficulty concentrating on the tasks. For example, the impaired driver may locate his or her driver's license, but forget the additional requests of producing a registration and certificate of insurance. Look for indications of decreased fine motor control in the form of difficulty in removing their license from a wallet or purse or sifting through papers in the glove compartment.

Rapid Follow Up Questions

After asking for a driver's license and while the subject is looking for the document, ask an additional question, such as "where have you been?" Again, this causes the subject to concentrate on multiple mental processes and/or physical skills. More often than not, the driver will stop looking for their license and answer the question, or continue to look for the license and disregard or forget the question.

Unusual Questions

NHTSA, in a third category of Pre-Exit testing techniques, advises asking "Unusual Questions." For example, after making contact with the driver and receiving requested documents, such as a driver's license, an officer might ask the subject, "In what year was your tenth birthday?" But be careful. These types of questions can cause confusion, and may falsely indicate an impaired condition. Further, this category of Pre-Exit test may bring about the sudden realization that he or she is in fact being tested. They may also object to a perceived unfairness on the part of the officer, and this perception may produce objections to any further roadside tests.

> **Pre-Exit tests are extremely valuable in that they test a driver's state of impairment while he or she is completely unaware, and therefore, will not mask or attempt to compensate for their intoxication. Because the subject is unaware of tests, however, care must be taken to make certain that they are valid. In other words, the tests must be conducted in a fair, impartial and professional manner.**

Admissions

At times, drivers may spontaneously admit to having consumed an alcoholic beverage and/or drugs. They may also state how much they have actually consumed. Record this admission! This type of evidence is completely admissible. Evidence obtained by an officer prior to the subject being placed under arrest and made at the time and place of an initial investigation is admissible in court.

Documentation

Note and detail any smells connected with the driver and the vehicle. Be certain of their origin. Document the manner in which the driver responds to questions or statements. Carefully observe the outward demeanor of the subject, i.e. clothing, eyes, skin tones, emotions, speech, walking and standing ability, ability or inability to locate a driver's license or other document, etc.

SECTION FOUR: Field Sobriety Testing (Standardized Field Sobriety Testing)

The traffic stop has been affected or an accident investigation has commenced, and the investigating officer observes preliminary characteristics of intoxication in one or more of the drivers. Satisfied that a DUI situation may exist, the investigation proceeds into a third step of conducting roadside Psycho-Physical examinations, or as they are commonly known, Field Sobriety Tests.

Basic courses stress recording what the subject "could or could not do," with regards to the performance of field sobriety tests. Of course, the simplicity of this type of report has its place within the investigative process. Experienced investigators can no longer be satisfied with this type of approach. In fact, they must delve deeper into why these outward manifestations of impairment occur. In this way, the trier of facts, prosecutors and defense attorney will view the officer as an expert and a peer within the judicial system.

In the third step of the investigative process, the subject is asked to exit the vehicle, and testing is conducted in or on an environment where the driver has no support other than his or her impaired or unimpaired mental and physical abilities. In other words, they are not seated within the vehicle; they cannot lean against the door or quarter panel. They are simply on their own to either "sink or swim."

Field Sobriety tests must be conducted on a clean, dry and level surface. If this type of environment is not available at the location of the stop, ask the subject to accompany you to another location where FST's can be accomplished in a safe and fair manner.

The important symptoms of impairment to look for include:
- Impaired Divided Attention
- Impaired Balance and Coordination
- Impaired Cognitive Thought Processes
- Impaired Vision
- Emotional Instability
- Nystagmus and other abnormal eye characteristics

The following are symptoms which are usually associated with impaired gross motor controls of a moderately intoxicated person.

- Difficulty in manipulating documents
- Difficulty in manipulating fingers while performing certain field sobriety tests
- Difficulty in manipulating devices within the vehicle interior, i.e., radio on/off switch

Examples of impaired gross motor controls of a severely intoxicated person:
- Difficulty in exiting the vehicle, i.e., leaning on the door to stand up.
- Difficulty or inability in standing or walking unassisted
  For example:
    Walking pigeon-toed
    Leaning on the side on the vehicle

Staggering

Falling

Weaving back and forth

- Inability to perform FST's as instructed and demonstrated

Important Notes: Keep in mind that even persons with low BAC levels may demonstrate the aforementioned visible symptoms of impaired motor controls.

It is important to understand and remember that alcohol and most other intoxicating substances act on the higher mental functions first. Lower functions are usually impaired at moderate to higher BAC's. If impaired balance and coordination are observed due to alcohol and/or drugs, then the investigator can be assured that the higher mental functions, such as judgment, are also impaired.

At low BAC levels, the thought processes of an individual are affected. The ability to form new ideas, process incoming information or communicate thoughts can be severely limited, even eliminated. For example, the driver will not be able to understand instructions for a Field Sobriety Test, or be able to express him or herself verbally. Their judgment is impaired.

They may ask the same questions repeatedly. For example, it is not uncommon for an arrested person to ask over and over again, "why am I under arrest?" Answers regarding DUI by the officer do not seem to satisfy them. Their cognitive thought processes are simply so impaired that they are unable to process the officer's answer.

Persons who are highly intoxicated will have obvious difficulty in focusing on objects. Double-vision is a common malady. Further, individuals may display the phenomenon wherein they appear to look straight through the investigator to an object behind; in other words, they will demonstrate an inability to focus on any one object and their eyes will appear to be glazed. Do not be fooled by redness of the sclera. This effect can be caused by too many other factors not connected with the Central Nervous System impairment.

> Officer Safety Issue

Remember that at relatively low BAC levels, the control of inhibitions are released, allowing emotions to be explicitly expressed when they would normally be held in check by the CNS. Also, the release of inhibitions allows normally suppressed hostilities to be vented in obviously inappropriate ways. This is certainly a cause for concern for all DUI investigators. Persons can appear to be very calm and suddenly become enraged and attack. Keep in mind that many people are upset when they are stopped and given a citation. This is normal; however, when some intoxicating substance releases the control over their inhibition and judgment, they can become emotional or enraged. Record these mood swings as important evidence of impairment.

Standardized Field Sobriety Tests Research and Development

The roadside field sobriety tests described in this manual are designed to assess whether or not there is:

- Divided Attention Impairment
- Impaired Balance and Coordination
- Impaired Cognitive Thought Processes

- Impaired Vision
- Emotional Instability
- Nystagmus and other Abnormal Eye Characteristics

An incredible amount of research and development has taken place in order to create what are now known as the Standardized Field Sobriety Tests and like any valid research; it was conducted in phases or steps. Conclusions were based on the proceeding phases.

The first phase of the research was conducted by THE SOUTHERN CALIFORNIA RESEARCH INSTITUTE. By BURNS, MARCELLINE and MOSKOWITZ. They wrote the final report, entitled Psycho-Physical Tests for DWI; June 1977, NHTSA report number DOT HS-802-424.

Initially, there were 238 volunteers who participated in one testing session. The volunteers were interviewed by SCRI staff members and on the basis of these interviews were classified as light, moderate or heavy drinkers. Thus, their tolerance level for alcohol consumption experience was determined. They were then assigned to target BAC levels appropriate to their drinking level classification.

During the laboratory portion of the study, ten police officers from three agencies in the metropolitan Los Angeles area participated in the testing. Each officer examined an average of 23 to 24 subjects. While the officers conducted the examinations, a member of the

SCRI staff observed. Neither the volunteers, the officers, nor the observers knew the volunteer's BAC. Separate SCRI staff members handled the dosing and breath testing of volunteers. The tests utilized, included the following:

1. One-Legged Stand
2. Finger to Nose
3. Finger Count
4. Walk and Turn
5. Racing
6. Nystagmus

Each officer was given one day of training in the administration and scoring of these tests prior to conducting the experiment.

The researchers analyzed their data and found that, using the scores from all six tests, they could correctly classify a volunteer's BAC as being either above or below .10 approximately 83% of the time. The researchers also found that this same level of reliability could be achieved just by considering the scores for the Nystagmus, Walk and Turn, and One-Leg Stand. In other words, those three tests constituted an 83% reliability battery for distinguishing BAC's of .10%.

The overall conclusions were that the three-test battery of Nystagmus, Walk and Turn, and One-Leg Stand clearly appeared to offer a very reliable Field Sobriety Testing procedure. These tests were not yet standardized or validated, however.

The second phase of the research included 296 volunteers in one testing session. 145 of these volunteers returned for a second session of the validation research.

For the laboratory portion of the second phase of the study, ten police officers from three agencies in the metropolitan Los Angeles area conducted the testing. Each officer examined an average of 44 subjects. While the officer conducted the examinations, a member of the SCRI staff observed. Again, neither the volunteers, or the officers or the observer knew the volunteer's BAC.

In the field portion of the study, participating officers were drawn from four stations of the Los Angeles County Sheriff's Office. They included a group called the "experimentals," who received training in the Standardized Field Sobriety Tests. There was also a control group, who did not receive training until the final stage of the study. Both groups were instructed to complete data forms for all of their traffic stops during the study period. In addition, SCRI researchers periodically rode with every officer to monitor their performance, and to insure that procedures were strictly adhered to.

Again, the SOUTHERN CALIFORNIA RESEARCH INSTITUTE conducted additional research to identify the feasibility and effectiveness of the three battery testing procedure.

The testing officers administered three tests:
1. Horizontal Gaze Nystagmus
2. Walk and Turn
3. One-Leg Stand

The results of the laboratory study demonstrated that the battery of three tests could be used reliably to distinguish subjects' with BAC's of .10 or more from those with lower BAC's. Collectively, the ten officers and two observers were correct in classifying subjects' BAC's, above or below .10, about 83% of the time. After publication of the SCRI report, NHTSA re-analyzed the laboratory data and found that the Nystagmus Test, by itself, could produce a 77% accurate classification. Similarly, Walk and Turn was capable of 68% unaided accuracy, and the One-Leg Stand of 65%. NHTSA also found that it would be possible to combine the results of the Nystagmus and Walk and Turn in a "decision matrix," and achieve 80% accuracy.

The SCRI reported a number of problems that plagued the field study. Among these was the lack of consistency by the participating officers in submitting data forms. SCRI concluded that the field test data would not support in-depth statistical analysis, but nevertheless disclosed some favorable trends:
- After training on the three test battery, officers tended to make more DUI/DWI arrests

  and
- Trained officers were more accurate in identifying suspects whose BAC's were above .10.

The overall conclusion of the study was that the test battery works well; nevertheless, it remained necessary to conduct a rigorous field test.

The objective of the field-testing was to:
- Develop standardized, practical and effective procedures for police officers to use in reaching arrest or no-arrest decisions;
- To test the feasibility of the procedures in operational conditions; and
- To secure data to determine if the tests will discriminate as well in the field as in the laboratory.

Validation

In support of the first of the objectives, the NHTSA research staff began by re-analyzing the SCRI data with a view toward systematization, the administration and scoring procedures for the three tests. Their intent was to ensure that the tests would be quick and easy to use, and that they could each be used independently of each other. For example, if the officer elected to use only one or two of the tests, they would maximize the detection of drivers with BAC's above .10 while minimizing the continued investigation of persons below that level. The current administrative and scoring procedures, and scoring criteria, for the three tests emerged from the re-analysis.

In late 1982 and early 1983, 1,506 drivers were stopped for suspicion of DWI by officers in four large areas in the eastern states. All participating officers completed a one-day training session prior to the beginning of the study. The training included practice in administering the tests to volunteer drinkers.

The officers used the three-test battery, but not all subjects were exposed to all three tests because circumstances of the stop location and/or the subject sometimes precluded the use of one or two of the tests. In fact, 89% of the subjects were examined using the Nystagmus test, 84% the Walk and Turn and 83% the One-Leg Stand.

All of the tests were standardized in the following manner:
- They were always administered in the same way;
- The officer administering the tests always looks for a specific set of clues on each test; and
- The officer always assessed a subject's performance against specific criteria for each test.

The importance of this large-scale field validation study deserves to be emphasized. It was the first significant assessment of the "workability" of the standardized tests under actual enforcement conditions, and it was the first time that completely objective clues and scoring criteria had been defined for the tests. The results of the study unmistakably validated the SFST's.

EXTREMELY IMPORTANT

This validation applies <u>only</u> when the tests are administered in the prescribed, standardized manner; and <u>only</u> when the

standardized clues are used to assess the subject's performance; and only when the standardized criteria are employed to interpret that performance. If any one of the standardized test elements is changed, the validity is compromised.

Elements Of The Standardized Field Sobriety Tests

The elements of the Standardized Field Sobriety Tests consist of:
- Standardized Administrative Procedures;
- Standardized Clues;
- Standardized Criterion.

Each of these elements will be described as the specific Field Sobriety Tests are discussed.

The final report citing the conclusion of the field test was written by:

> T., Schweitz, R. and Snyder, M., Field Evaluation of a Behavioral Test Battery for DWI, September 1983, NHTSA Report Number DOT HS-806 475.

It was found that the three battery tests were found to be highly reliable in identifying subjects whose BAC's were .10 or more. Considered independently, the Nystagmus test was the most accurate of the three among subjects who exhibit four or more clues. 82% had BAC's of .10 or higher. The other two tests were nearly as accurate, however. Combining the Nystagmus Test with the Walk and Turn showed an 83% of the subjects were classified correctly.

HORIZONTAL GAZE NYSTAGMUS TEST

Physiological Overview

Nystagmus is defined as minute jerking of the eyes. This is a "cerebeller" response to an injured or disabled cerebellum and the motor areas of the cerebrum. Within the context of the impaired driver, alcohol consumption or ingestion of certain other Central Nervous System depressants, inhalants or phencyclidine hinders the ability of the brain to correctly control eye muscles. The eye is observed to jerk or bounce.

The disablement in this case is caused by alcohol and/or drug toxicity. Horizontal Gaze Nystagmus testing has become a very useful tool in evaluating a person's degree of Central Nervous System impairment. That is to say, the earlier the onset of nystagmus, in terms of the angle measured from straight forward (0^0 angle) to maximum deviation (approximately 63^0) can quite accurately depict impairment.

Despite the strong correlation between alcohol consumption and HGN, some trial courts across the country still do not admit the results of the HGN test into evidence. Although there is scientific evidence to prove this correlation exists, lack of knowledge and inadequate preparation or limited proffers has caused the evidence presented to courts to be found insufficient to satisfy the evidentiary standards for admitting scientific or technical evidence. Consequently, law enforcement officers in a number of jurisdictions use the HGN test only for purposes of establishing probable cause, without securing admission of the test results into evidence at trial. Ultimately, the fact-finder never hears the results of the most reliable field sobriety test.

Legal and law enforcement communities need to better understand that HGN is the most reliable and effective indicator of alcohol impairment, and that ample evidence is available to prove reliability. The challenge is in conveying the strong correlation between the HGN test and impairment to the fact-finder, and showing how to effectively use the available evidence to prove the HGN test's validity and reliability in court.

Science

As stated before, Nystagmus is a term used to describe a "bouncing" eye motion that is displayed in two ways:

1. Pendular Nystagmus, where the eye oscillates equally in two directions

    and

2. Jerk Nystagmus, where the eye moves slowly away from a fixation point and then rapidly corrects through a "saccadic" or fast movement.

HGN is a type of "jerk" nystagmus with the saccadic movement toward the direction of the gaze. An eye normally moves smoothly like a marble rolling over a glass pane; whereas, an eye with jerk nystagmus moves like a marble on sandpaper. Most types of nystagmus, including HGN, are involuntary motions, and the person exhibiting the nystagmus cannot control it or, in fact, even be aware of it.

Alcohol and Nystagmus

There are several types of nystagmus. Alcohol causes two types: alcohol gaze nystagmus, which includes HGN, and positional alcohol nystagmus. Although alcohol causes both, alcohol gaze nystagmus and positional alcohol nystagmus are very different and easily distinguishable. Testing for positional alcohol nystagmus is not a part of the Standardized Field Sobriety Test battery. Defendants sometimes claim or attempt to confuse matters by arguing that the nystagmus the officer saw was actually positional alcohol nystagmus and not alcohol gaze nystagmus.

Alcohol Gaze Nystagmus

As stated before, Gaze Nystagmus is a type of "jerk" nystagmus where the eye gazing upon or following an object begins to lag, and has to correct itself with a saccadic movement toward the direction in which the eye is moving or gazing. Gaze Nystagmus is

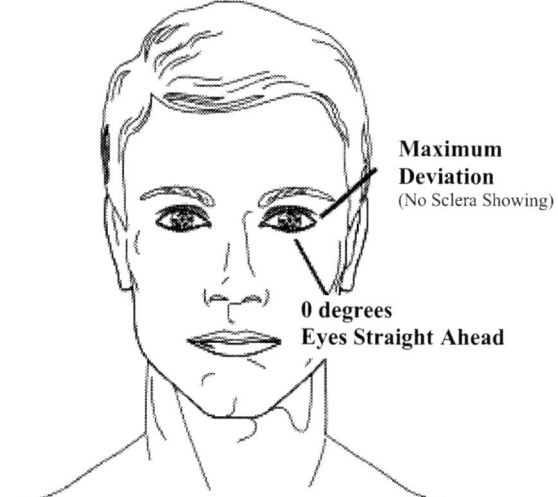

Figure 11: Testing Gaze

caused by disruptions within the nervous system. As mentioned in a previous section of this manual, alcohol and other drugs interfere with the normal functioning of the synaptic junctions. In particular, those functioning within the cerebellum, thalamus and hypothalamus, which play primary roles in governing the normal muscle functioning.

Gaze nystagmus occurs as the eye moves from looking straight-ahead (resting nystagmus), to the side (HGN), or up (Vertical nystagmus or VGN). Alcohol is a Central Nervous System depressant, affecting many of the higher as well as lower motor control systems of the body. This results in poor motor coordination, sluggish reflexes and emotional instability. The part of the nervous system that fine tunes and controls hand movements and body posture also controls eye movement. When intoxicated, a person's nervous system will display a breakdown in the smooth and accurate control of the eye movements. This breakdown may result in the inability to hold the eyes steady, resulting in a number of observable changes of impaired oculomotor functioning.

Horizontal Gaze Nystagmus provides the best evidence that the defendant ingested alcohol or other drugs. The HGN test provides the best evidence, however, only if the Trier of Fact understands that the results correlate with a degree of impairment.

Several issues may affect the admissibility of HGN test results:

1. Whether the Horizontal Gaze Nystagmus test is characterized as scientific or as an observation of a physical trait;
2. If HGN is deemed scientific, whether it is reliable;
3. Whether the law enforcement officer is properly trained to administer the HGN test;
4. Whether the officer properly administered the test in the particular case; and
5. The purpose for which the HGN test result will be used.

Jurisdictions treat the HGN test in one of two ways:

1. As an observation of a physical characteristic, the same as other Field Sobriety tests; and/or
2. As scientific evidence.

Horizontal Gaze Nystagmus as a Physical Characteristic

Some state courts have taken this position and held that the HGN test is similar to the other two Standardized Tests. That is, HGN is a physical manifestation of alcohol impairment, like a staggering gait, that can be readily observed by a law enforcement officer. These courts found that the HGN test is objective in nature and does not require expert interpretation, just like the Walk and Turn and the One-Leg Stand Tests. These courts also distinguish the

HGN test from scientific tests, such as the polygraph, in that the Horizontal Gaze Nystagmus test does not require a measuring or recording instrument.

To qualify the HGN test as a physical observation, the prosecution should show that the test operates on the same physiological principles as the other SFST's, i.e., alcohol impairs muscle control. The only foundation required is a showing of the officer's training and experience in administering the test and a showing that the test was properly administered. The law enforcement officer must establish his or her proficiency in conducting the test in order to make the correct observations. To do this, the law enforcement officer testifies about his or her training and experience with the HGN test (e.g., When and where trained? How many classroom hours? Did the officer perform the test on sober and impaired subjects in the classroom, and how many times? How many times has the officer given the HGN test in the field?). The officer must also testify that the HGN test was properly administered in accordance with his or her training. In other words, the prosecutor lays the same foundation as if the officer was testifying about the Walk and Turn or One-Leg Stand test. With that foundation, the HGN test results are admissible as evidence of impairment. The prosecutor may also argue that it is common knowledge that alcohol affects muscle control, based on the physical observations of the suspect.

While no expert testimony is needed to get the HGN test admitted into evidence at trial, as a practical matter, some demonstration to the Trier of Fact of the HGN test's reliability as an indicator of impairment may be needed. When the HGN test is admitted as a physical observation, the law enforcement officer can establish this reliability. The officer should explain that, based on training and experience in the interpretation and administration of the HGN test on impaired subjects, he or she can accurately identify that a subject is impaired when certain characteristics are noted during the Horizontal Gaze Nystagmus test. For example, the officer can testify that he or she has observed people impaired by alcohol on many occasions and in various settings, and has noted a strong correlation between alcohol consumption and HGN. To be persuasive to the Trier of Fact at trial, the officer should take the opportunity to communicate evidence of the HGN test's reliability. The significance of the HGN test, as the most reliable of the Standardized Field Sobriety Tests, for alcohol impairment will be lost otherwise.

Determination of HGN as a Scientific Test

The majority of state courts hold that the HGN test is a scientific test, resting upon the principle that there is a relationship between alcohol consumption and HGN, rather than it simply being an observation or common knowledge. In jurisdictions, where there are no appellate decisions with regards to the HGN test evidence, trial courts make the determination of whether the HGN test meets certain evidentiary standards, and the Trier of Fact must accept the test. Initially, the trial court has the role of "gatekeeper."

In performing its role as "gatekeeper," the trial court ensures that the Trier of Fact does not attach an undue aura of reliability to "scientific" evidence that is not scientifically valid. Evidence that purports to be based on science beyond the common knowledge of the average person that does not meet the judicial standard for scientific validity can mislead, confuse and mystify the jury. See *Hawkins v. State*, 476 S.E.2d 803, 808-09 (Ga. Ct App. 1996). Procedurally, the trial court may perform this "gatekeeper" role by holding an evidentiary hearing. At that hearing, it is within the discretion of the trial court to determine what scientific evidence the jury will hear.

The two most common evidentiary standards for scientific evidence are:

1. The *Frye* Standard
   and
2. The Federal Rules of Evidence or the *Daubert* standard.

The standard a court applies depends on the law of the individual jurisdiction. The primary purpose of each of these standards is to ensure that the evidence is reliable and not junk science.

Frye **Standard**

In 1923, the Court of Appeals for the District of Columbia held in *Frye v. United States* that for new or novel scientific evidence to be admissible, it must "have gained general acceptance in the particular field in which it belongs." This standard came to be known as the *Frye* standard.

It should be noted that testing for Nystagmus also allows an officer to inspect the eyes for vital indications of other brain injury or disease not associated with alcohol or drugs. This scientific test will be described at length later in this section. Technically, there are two prongs to the *Frye* standard:

1. Identifying the "particular field" or relevant scientific community

   and

2. Demonstrating that novel scientific evidence (such as the HGN test) is generally accepted in that community.

Combined, both prongs provide a measure of the reliability of the scientific evidence.

In 1986 in the case of *State v. Superior Court (Blake)*, the Arizona Supreme Court examined which fields of science constituted the relevant scientific community required by *Frye* before determining that the HGN test was generally accepted in that community. The court first found that *"the work of highway safety professionals and behavioral psychologists who study effects of alcohol on behavior is directly affected by the claims and application of the Horizontal Gaze Nystagmus test, so that both these groups must be included in the "relevant scientific community."* The court also found that the relevant scientific community should include the fields of neurology and criminalistics, but to a lesser degree because neither of those fields focus specifically on HGN and alcohol. Other courts have agreed with the *State v. Superior Court* conclusions.

One or more witnesses must be called regarding general acceptance in the relevant community. Before any witness can testify about general acceptance, however, the court must qualify the witness as an expert. There is no bright line test under *Frye* governing when a court must qualify a witness as an expert. The expert must impart to the jury knowledge within the scope of the expert's special skill and experience that is otherwise unavailable to the jury from other sources. Courts measure the quality of the witness's special skill and experience in terms of years of study and work experience, degrees and other accolades received, research performed and publications written, among other things.

It is important to point out that although evidence may rest on scientific principles, *Frye* only applies to scientific evidence that is "new or novel." At least one state court that applied a relevancy standard for determining the admissibility of scientific evidence found that the HGN test was not novel for the purpose of showing some indication of alcohol. This same court admitted the HGN test in conjunction with the results of the other SFST's. This is a minority position, however. *Whitson v. State*, 863 S.W. 2d 794, 798 (Ark. 1993).

Federal Rules of Evidence (*Daubert* Standard)

In 1993, the United States Supreme Court held in *Daubert v. Merrill Dow Pharmaceuticals, Inc.* that the Federal Rules of Evidence, specifically Rule 702, replaced the common law Frye standard as the evidentiary basis for admitting scientific evidence in Federal Courts. The Supreme Court found that Rule 702 does not incorporate the general acceptance requirement of the Frye standard as a prerequisite for the admission of expert scientific testimony. The result is a more liberal standard, which allows the Trier of Fact to hear scientific evidence conditioned upon testimony indicating that the evidence to be admitted is both relevant to the issues involved at trial and reliable.

Meeting the Scientific Standard of the Jurisdiction

To date, the courts have determined the HGN evidence does meet *Frye* and is, therefore, admissible at trial, with one exception. Some courts have held that the prosecution failed to present evidence sufficient for the trial court to make findings as to the scientific reliability of the HGN test. In these cases, the prosecution generally relied solely on the testimony of the arresting officer to establish the reliability of the HGN test.

Frye requires the proponent of the evidence to prove general acceptance in the relevant scientific community. In *Daubert*, the Court stated in dicta that evidence that satisfied *Frye* would also satisfy the requirements of FRE 702. Cases that hold that the HGN test is scientifically reliable under *Frye,* therefore, are relevant under the FRE.

Summary

Impaired driving detection and prosecution has improved since the initial 1977 NHTSA study, due in large part to the use of the SFST battery by law enforcement on the street and prosecutors in the courtroom. Efforts to reduce impaired driving in many parts of the United States, however, could not fully benefit from administering the SFST battery because of the exclusion of the HGN test from some impaired driving trials. The effectiveness of the SFST battery to curb impaired driving cannot be achieved to its full potential unless all of the three tests are utilized throughout the country.

Other Forms of Nystagmus

It is not uncommon for defense attorneys to bring up, in an attempt to confuse the Trier of Fact, the many varieties of Nystagmus that can be found with the human being.

The following are the most common forms of Nystagmus which have nothing to do with the investigation of a DUI offense:

- **Rotational Nystagmus** – occurs when the head or body is spinning.
- **Post-Rotational Nystagmus** – occurs after the head or body has stopped spinning. The direction of the fast-phase bouncing will be opposite direction of the spinning.
- **Caloric Nystagmus** – occurs when fluid motion in the canals of the vestibular system is stimulated by temperature. This can be observed when warm water is placed in one ear and cold in the other ear.

- **Positional Alcohol Nystagmus** – occurs when the gravity of the blood is altered and is in unequal concentrations in the blood and vestibular system. This makes the vestibular system responsive to gravity in certain positions.
- **Optokinetic Nystagmus** – this is observed within the majority of the population. It occurs when the eyes follow an object out of view (panning across a horizontal plane). A person who is riding on a train demonstrates an example of this. The person watches as stationary objects pass by. Their eyes will not move smoothly, but instead, jerk as they follow the object across the visual field.
- **Physiologic Nystagmus** – is also a naturally-occurring phenomenon. It occurs when the eyes move from side to side. Again, the eyes do not move smoothly; instead, they move in a series of jerks. It is believed that the eyes move in this manner to keep the muscles from becoming fatigued.
- **Aural Nystagmus** – due to disturbances in the vestibular labyrinth.
- **Cheyne-Stokes Nystagmus** – a particular rhythmical eye movement, resembling Cheyne-Stokes respiration.
- **Disassociative Nystagmus** – movement of both eyes different from each other. One has vertical movement, while the other has horizontal movement.
- **Disjunctive Nystagmus** – both eyes swing toward or away from each other.
- **Fixation Nystagmus** – rapid movement of the eyes when gazing at a stationary object.

- **Head Nystagmus** – oscillatory movement of the eyes when the head moves.
- **Labyrinthine Nystagmus** – see Vestibular Nystagmus.
- **Latent Nystagmus** – occurs only when one eye is covered.
- **Miners Nystagmus** – an occupational disease of coal miners consisting of abnormal eye movements due to poor lighting.
- **Occular-Nystagmus** – due to eye disease.
- **Optokinetic Nystagmus** – due to looking at a stationary object from a moving platform or vice versa.
- **Oscillating Nystagmus** – undulating Nystagmus
- **Palatal Nystagmus** – occurs when there are involuntary muscle contractions. In this case, it has to do with the eyes, usually associated with convulsive disorders.
- **Panoptic Nystagmus** – false Nystagmus, occurring when there is a weakness of the occular muscles.
- **Pendular Nystagmus** – slow back and forth movement of the eyes. See Undulating Nystagmus.
- **Railroad Nystagmus** – Optokinetic Nystagmus.
- **Retraction Nystagmus/Retractory Nystagmus** – a spasmodic backward retraction of the eyeball. It is associated with diseases of the midbrain. It consists of slow movement in one direction, followed by a rapid return movement in the opposite direction. See Jerking Nystagmus.
- **Rhythmical Nystagmus** – See Retraction Nystagmus.
- **Rotary Nystagmus** – nystagmus noted while eye is in a circular movement.
- **Undulating Nystagmus** – consists of to and fro movements of equal velocity.

- **Unilateral Nystagmus** – nystagmus in only one eye.
- **Vestibular Nystagmus** – nystagmus caused by vestibular disturbance usually with internal ear problems. See Labyrinthine Nystagmus.
- **Vibratory Nystagmus** – see Undulatory Nystagmus.
- **Visual Nystagmus** – characterized by smooth pendulum like movements of the eyes.

> **It has been found that 3% to 4% of the population has a natural Nystagmus at an earlier onset than at the normal maximum deviation; therefore, an investigating officer should never solely rely on HGN in making their decision to arrest for DUI.**

HORIZONTAL GAZE NYSTAGMUS TESTING

The Gaze Nystagmus test, which an officer conducts at the roadside, is a test of either or both Horizontal and Vertical Gaze Nystagmus. For example, the Nystagmus occurs either in a horizontal plane or under certain circumstances in a vertical plane.

Most individuals will always have a slight Nystagmus at the maximum deviation; that is, the eyes are turned, either fully left or right. With intoxication by alcohol and certain narcotic drugs, however, three very distinct signs will be observed:

1. **The subject cannot follow a slowly, smoothly moving object with the eyes.** Instead, the eyes will jerk or bounce as they move left or right in pursuit of the stimulus, such as a finger, penlight or writing pen.

2. **When the subject follows the stimulus, right or left, to their maximum deviation and held in this position momentarily, a distinct jerking will be evident.**
3. **The more intoxicated a person becomes, the less the eyes have to move towards the side or upwards, in the case of vertical Nystagmus, to indicate impairment.**

PROCEDURES FOR HORIZONTAL GAZE NYSTAGMUS TEST

Horizontal Gaze Nystagmus Standardized Administrative Procedures

- Hold a stimulus 12–15 inches in front of the subject's face;
- Keep the tip of the stimulus slightly above the subjects eyes;
- Always move the stimulus smoothly;
- Always check for three cues in both eyes;
- Check the clues in this sequence:
    1. Lack of smooth pursuit
    2. Distinct Nystagmus at maximum deviation
    3. Onset of Nystagmus prior to 45^0
    4. Always check for each clue at least twice in each eye.

Horizontal Gaze Nystagmus Standardized Clues

- Lack of smooth pursuit;
- Distinct Nystagmus at maximum deviation;
- Onset of Nystagmus prior to 45^0.

Important Note → No other clues are recognized by NHTSA as valid indicators of Horizontal Gaze Nystagmus. In particular, NHTSA does not support the allegation that onset angle can reliably be used to estimate BAC levels. **Any such estimation is a misuse of the Horizontal Gaze Nystagmus test.**

Horizontal Gaze Nystagmus Standardized Criterion

The maximum number of clues for Horizontal Gaze Nystagmus that a subject can exhibit is six. This occurs when all three cues are observed in both eyes. If the subject exhibits four or more clues, it should be considered evidence that they are under the influence of alcohol or drugs.

Step One

- **Begin by asking the subject whether he or she is wearing hard contact lenses. If the subject is wearing contact lenses, note the fact, but do not request them to be removed.** The lenses do not interfere with the testing procedure and may be a liability issue. Removing the lenses could be difficult for an intoxicated individual, and may cause injury to their eyes or loss of the lenses.

- **Ask the subject if he or she is blind in either eye, or have a glass eye in either socket.** If either condition exists, do not attempt HGN testing.

- **If the subject is wearing eyeglasses, instruct him or her to remove them.**

Step Two

Give the following instructions, verbatim, from a position of interrogation and remember officer survival skills. Always have an assisting officer present.

- **I am going to check your eyes.**
- **Keep your head still, and follow this (show them the object which will be used to conduct the test).**
- **Keep focusing on this, and follow it with your eyes until I tell you to stop.**
- **Ask the subject if they understand.** If not, restate the instructions, and note the impaired cognitive thought processes.

Keep the stimulus approximately 12" to 15" in front of the face. Move it in a horizontal motion when checking the eyes. Check the subject's left eye by moving the stimulus to the right. Move it in such a manner that it requires approximately three to four seconds to bring the subject's eye as far as it will go, which is known as the maximum deviation. While moving the stimulus, look at the subject's eyeball and determine whether it is able to pursue smoothly. Do not hesitate to make two or more passes in front of the eye in order to be sure.

After the first eye has been checked for smooth pursuit, or more importantly, the lack of smooth pursuit, check the same eye for distinct Nystagmus at maximum deviation. No sclera (white of the eye) will be showing in the corner of the eyeball nearest the ear. It is important that the eye be held at maximum deviation for 2 to 3 seconds.

After checking the eye at maximum deviation, look for the angle of onset of Nystagmus in the same eye. Move the stimulus back to 0^0 or straight ahead, and then slowly move back towards a 45^0 angle. As the stimulus is moved, watch for the onset of Nystagmus. If Nystagmus is noted, stop the stimulus and wait for a moment to see if the Nystagmus is distinct. If well-defined Nystagmus is noted at a specific angle, note the angle to determine the angle of onset. If Nystagmus is not observed, keep moving the stimulus until Nystagmus is noted, or the 45^0 angle is reached. It is important to note whether the angle of onset is at or before the 45^0 angle. **Do not use the criteria of 45^0 angle of onset, unless sclera is showing on the side of the eye towards the ear.**

1. **Check for smooth or lack of smooth pursuit.**
2. **Check for HGN at maximum deviation.**
3. **Check for the angle of onset of HGN.**

Repeat the procedures for the other eye.

Step Three
Scoring HGN Test

There are three possible signs of intoxication for each eye. Score one point for each symptom checked, for a maximum of six points.

1. **Lack of smooth pursuit in the left eye.**
2. **Nystagmus in the left eye at maximum deviation is distinct.**
3. **Onset of Horizontal Gaze Nystagmus in the left eye occurs at or before 45^0.** Do not score this

symptom unless sclera is visible on the outside edge of the left eye at the point of onset.

4. **Lack of smooth pursuit in the right eye.**
5. **Nystagmus in the right eye at maximum deviation is distinct.**
6. **Onset of Horizontal Gaze Nystagmus in the right eye occurs at or before 45⁰.** Do not score this symptom unless sclera is visible on the outside edge of the right eye.

If the subject scores four or more points out of the six possible, classify his or her BAC as impairing.

Testing Conditions

Very few test conditions will affect gaze Nystagmus. The subject should be taken out of inclement weather in order to assure a fair and accurate test result.

> **Vertical Nystagmus is not a standardized test, but is nevertheless very useful in determining whether or not a subject is intoxicated by stimulants and hallucinogens. The test is conducted in the same manner as HGN Testing.**

Summary

Nystagmus can be observed easily, without the use for special equipment; nevertheless, there is a need for a stimulus, such as finger, pen, or penlight, which the subject can follow with the eyes. As stated before, the stimulus should be held above the level of the eyes. This will assure that the subject's eyes are wide open when they look at the object.

> **NOTE:** Nystagmus may be caused by situational factors other than alcohol. These include the ingestion of (PCP), barbiturates and other depressants. In addition, a large disparity between the performance of the right and left eye may indicate brain damage. This is particularly important if a traffic accident has occurred.

PROCEDURES FOR WALK AND TURN TEST

Walk and Turn Standardized Administrative Procedures

Always begin by having the subject assume the heel to toe stance.

- Verify that the subject understands that the stance is to be maintained while the instructions are given.
- If the subject breaks away from the stance as the instructions are given, cease giving instructions until the stance is returned.
- Tell the subject that they will be required to take 9 heel to toe steps down the line, to turn, and to take 9 heel to toe steps up the line.
- Demonstrate several heel to toe steps and a turn.
- Tell the subject to keep their arms at the sides.
- Tell them to watch their feet.
- Tell them to count steps out loud.
- Tell them to not stop walking until the test is completed.
- Ask the subject whether they understand.
- If not, re-explain what is not understood.
- Tell the subject to begin.

- If the subject staggers or stops, allow them to resume from the point of interruption.
- Do not require the subject to start over from the beginning.

Walk and Turn Standardized Clues

1. Loses balance during the instructions
2. Starts walking too soon
3. Stops while walking
4. Misses heel to toe while walking
5. Raises arms from side while walking
6. Steps off the line
7. Turns improperly
8. Takes wrong number of steps

These eight are the only validated clues of Walk and Turn. Officers may see or hear other noteworthy evidence while the subject is performing this test, however, and any additional observations should be included in their report, but should not be included with the observations made during the test.

In addition, officers should note in their report how many times each of the eight clues appears. For purposes of applying the standardized criterion, a clue should be counted only once, even if it appears more than once.

Walk and Turn Standardized Criterion

If the subject cannot perform or complete the test, it should be counted as exhibiting nine clues. One situation that would warrant this is if the subject steps off the line three or more times.

If the subject exhibits at least two clues on the Walk and Turn, it should be considered evidence that they may be under the influence of alcohol and/or drugs.

Step One

Initial Positioning and Verbal Instructions

Have the subject assume the heel to toe stance by giving verbal instructions, accompanied by demonstration:

- **Place your left foot on the line (Demonstrate)**
- **Place your right foot on the line ahead of the left foot, with the heel of the right against the toes of the left foot. (Demonstrate).**
- **Hold this position until told to start walking. Do not start walking until told to do so.**
- **Do you understand the instructions so far?** (Make sure that the subject indicates that he or she understands the instructions to this point. Repeat the instructions, and note the impaired cognitive thought process.)

Step Two
Demonstration and Instructions for the Walking Stage

Explain the test requirements, using the following verbal instructions, accompanied by demonstration:

- **When I tell you to start, take nine heel to toe steps down the line, turn around, and take nine heel to toe steps back up the line.**
- **When you turn, keep the front foot on the line, and turn by taking a series of small steps with the other foot. (Demonstrate the turn).**
- **While you are walking, keep your arms at your sides, watch your feet at all times, and count your steps out loud. (Demonstrate the several heel to toe steps.)**
- **Once you start walking, don't stop until you have completed the test.**
- **Do you understand the instruction? (Make sure the subject indicates he or she understands. If not understood, repeat the instructions and note the lack of cognitive thought process).**
- **Begin, and count your first step from the heel to toe position as "one."**

An investigator may observe a number of different behaviors when a subject performs this test. Research has demonstrated that the behaviors listed below are most likely observed in someone with a BAC of .10% or more. In scoring this test, give only one point for each item observed (even if the item is observed more than once,) with a maximum score of nine points.

Step Three
Scoring Walk and Turn Test

- **Cannot keep balance while listening to the instructions.** Two tasks are required at the beginning of this test. The subject must balance heel to toe on the line, and at the same time listen carefully to the instructions. Typically, the person, who is intoxicated, can accomplish only one of these tasks. He or she may listen to the instructions, but be unable to keep their balance. Score this item if the subject does not maintain the heel to toe position throughout the instructions. Do not score this item if the subject sways or uses the arms to balance, but maintains the heel to toe position.

- **Starts before the instructions are finished.** The intoxicated person may also keep balance, but not listen to the instructions. Since the investigator will have specifically told the subject not to start until told to do so, score this item if the subject does not wait.

- **Stops while walking to steady themselves.** The subject pauses for several seconds after one or more steps. Do not score this item if the subject is merely walking slowly.

- **Does not touch heel to toe on each step.** The subject leaves a space of 1/2 inch or more between heel and toe. Additionally, score this item if the subject does not walk in a straight line.

- **Steps off the line.** Score this item if the subject steps entirely off the line. Count this item once, although the subject steps off the line several times.
- **Uses arms to balance.** The subject raises one or both arms more than six inches from their sides in order to maintain balance.
- **Loses balance while turning.** The subject removes the pivot foot from the line while turning. That is, score this item if both feet are removed from the line. Also, score this item if both feet are removed from the line, or have clearly not followed direction in turning. For example, the subject pivots in one step, rather than several small steps.
- **Incorrect number of steps.** Score this item if the subject takes more or fewer than the nine steps in either direction.
- **Cannot do the test.** Score this item if the subject steps off the line three or more times, is in danger of falling, or otherwise demonstrates that he or she cannot do the test. In scoring this item, the subject gets the maximum of 9 points.

Should the subject have difficulty with the test (for example steps off the line) have him or her repeat the test from the point of difficulty, not from the beginning.

This test tends to lose its sensitivity if it is repeated several times. Observe the subject from three to four feet away, and remain motionless while the subject attempts the test. Being too close or moving excessively will make it more difficult for the subject to accomplish the test. If the subject scores two or more points on this test, classify his or her BAC as impairing. Using this criteria, an investigator will be able to classify about 69% of subjects with respect to being impaired. The decision point on the walk and turn test is two.

Test Conditions

The walk and turn test requires a hard, dry, level and non-slip surface, with room for the subject to complete nine heel-to-toe steps. A straight line must be clearly visible on the surface. Conditions must be such that the subject will not be in danger if he or she were to fall.

Decision Table

The decision table (Figure 12) was designed to help an officer classify those subjects with a potential of .10 % or more. You will recall that the decision point for the Gaze Nystagmus Test was a score of four, while the decision point for the Walk and Turn is two points.

If the subject, however, were to score high on one test and low on the other how would a decision be made? Find the box on the decision table where the two scores intersect, and see if it falls within the

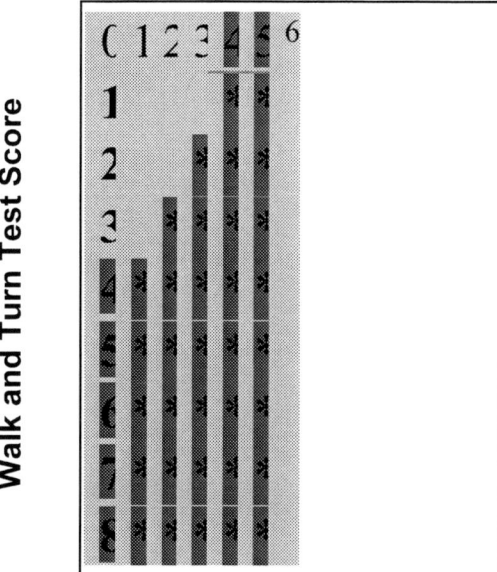

Figure 12: Decision Table

shaded area. If the combined scores are located in the shaded area, the subject is probably impaired.

It is very important to remember that "probable cause" is developed by looking at the entire picture. The DUI investigator must evaluate the Driving Pattern, Physical Demeanor along with the Field Sobriety Tests.

PROCEDURES FOR THE ONE-LEG STAND
One-Leg Stand Standardized Administrative Procedures

1. Tell the subject to stand with feet together, and arms at sides
2. Tell the subject not to start the test until you say to do so
3. Ask the subject if he/she understands

4. Tell the subject to stand on one foot, with the other foot held straight about six inches off the ground, toes pointed forward and parallel to the ground
5. Demonstrate the stance
6. Tell the subject to count from 1 to 30, by thousands
7. Demonstrate the count, for several seconds
8. Ask the subject whether he/she understand; if not, re-explain whatever is not understood
9. Tell the subject to begin
10. If the subject stops or puts the foot down, allow him/her to resume at the point of interruption; do not require the count to begin again.

One-Leg Stand Standardized Clues
1. Sways
2. Puts foot down
3. Hops
4. Raises arms from side, six inches or more

Officers may see or hear other noteworthy evidence while the subject is performing this test, and any additional observations should be included in their report.

If the subject cannot perform or complete the test, it should be counted as having exhibited five clues. One situation that would warrant this is if the subject puts the foot down three or more times.

One-Leg Stand Criterion

If the subject exhibits two or more clues the One-leg Stand, it should be considered evidence that they are under the influence. As with the Walk and Turn, clues should be counted only once in applying this criterion.

Step One

Instruction Stage and Initial Positioning

Initiate the test by giving the following verbal instructions, accompanied by demonstration:

- **Please stand with your heels together and your arms down at your sides. (Demonstrate)**
- **Do not start to perform the test until told to do so.**
- **Do you understand the instructions so far? (Make sure the subject indicates that he or she understands, if not, repeat the instructions and note the impaired cognitive thought processes).**

Step Two

Balancing and Counting Stage

Explain the test requirements, using the verbal instructions below, accompanied by demonstration:

- **When told to start, stand on one leg, holding the other foot out in front. (Demonstrate)**
- **You may stand on either leg that you wish.**
- **Keep the raised foot about six inches off the ground. (Demonstrate)**

- While you are standing, count aloud for 30 seconds. (Demonstrate a count as follows. One thousand one, one thousand two, one thousand three, and so on, until one thousand 30.)
- Throughout the entire test, keep your arms at the sides at all times, and keep watching the raised foot. (Demonstrate)
- Do not hop or sway while standing.
- Do you understand? Go ahead and perform the test.

Step Three
Scoring One-Leg Stand

Researchers have found that those behaviors listed below are most likely to be observed in someone with a BAC of .10% or higher. In scoring this test, give one point for each item observed, even if it noted more than once. The decision point for the One-leg Stand is two.

- **The subject sways while balancing.** (This refers to side to side or back and forth motions, while the subject maintains the one-leg stand).
- **Uses arms for balance.** (He or she moves the arms six or more inches from the side of the body in order to keep balance.)
- **Hopping.** The subject is able to keep one foot off the ground, but resorts to hopping on the anchor foot in order to maintain balance.

- **Puts foot down.** (The subject is not able to maintain the one-leg stand position, putting the foot down one or more times.)
- **Cannot do the test.** (Score this item if the subject puts the foot down three or more times during the 30-second count or otherwise demonstrates that he or she cannot do the test.) If the investigator must score this item, give the maximum amount of points (5).

Remember that time is critical in this test. Research has shown that a person with a BAC of .10% can maintain balance for up to 25 seconds, but seldom as long as 30 seconds.

If an individual scores two or more points on the One-Leg Stand, there is a good chance that the subject is impaired. Using this criterion, an investigator can correctly classify about 65% of the people tested as either above or below .10 %.

If the subject puts his/her foot down, instruct him or her to pick up the foot again and continue counting from the point at which the foot touched the ground. If the subject counts very slowly, terminate the test after 30 seconds have actually elapsed.

Test Conditions

The One-Leg Stand requires a hard, dry, level and non-slip surface. There should be adequate lighting for the subject to have some visual frame of reference, and conditions must be such that the subject will be in no danger if he or she were to fall. Observe the subject from at least three feet away, and remain as motionless as possible while he or she is performing the test.

Although the Standardized Field Sobriety Tests are the most scientifically proven way of determining impairment, there will be occasions when the investigating officer will have to substitute tests in order to adapt to the situation. Mental and physical handicaps may preclude the use of certain tests. Fairness is the key issue here. Other tests, besides the Standardized Field Sobriety Test Battery, can be used, such as the Modified Rhomberg, or the Finger Count Test. Remember that it takes both mental and physical abilities, working in tandem, to operate a motor vehicle. Both these aspects in combination must be examined, at the same time, with each test.

ALTERNATE FIELD SOBRIETY TESTS

The following Field Sobriety Tests are not among the scientifically validated tests known as Standardized Field Sobriety Tests. There are no decision points. Their significance as "Divided Attention" tests, however, is uncannily accurate and extremely valuable substitutes for any of the other tests.

PROCEDURES FOR THE MODIFIED RHOMBERG TEST
Step One
Instruction Stage and Initial Positioning
Explain the initial instructions in the following manner:
- **When told to do so, stand with your heels and toes together, your arms down at your side. (Demonstrate)**

- Close your eyes, tilt your head backwards, (Demonstrate) and listen to the remainder of the instructions.
- **Do you understand?** (Make sure the subject indicates that he or she understands; if not, repeat the instructions and note the impaired cognitive thought processes).
- Go ahead, take the initial position.

Step Two

Instruction, Balancing and Counting Stage

While the subject is balancing in the initial position explain the following:

- While you are balancing, you must determine when 30 seconds have elapsed from the time you are told to begin.
- When you believe that 30 seconds has elapsed, tilt your head down and look straight ahead. You may count silently to yourself if you wish.
- **Do you understand?** (Make sure the subject indicates that he or she understands, if not, repeat the instructions and note the impaired cognitive thought processes).

While the subject is mentally calculating when 30 seconds have elapsed, utilize a stopwatch or the second hand of a wristwatch to determine when the time has actually elapsed. If the subject is intoxicated on CNS depressants, their determination of 30 seconds will be longer. If they are intoxicated on a CNS stimulant, their determination of 30 seconds will be shorter than the actual 30-second interval.

Step Three
Scoring Modified Rhomberg Test
Score one point for each of the following items:
- **Required additional instruction during the test.**
- **Opened eyes during the test.**
- **Failed to keep heels and together during the test.**
- **Failed to keep head tilted back.**
- **Swayed more than 4 inches off center, side-to-side or front to back. A figure-8 motion may also be observed.**
- **More than 10-second difference in the time.**
- **Unable to do the test. If the subject is in danger of falling over or, for whatever reason, in not able to accomplish the test, score a total of 7 points.**

Test Conditions
The Modified Rhomberg Test requires a hard, dry, level, non-slip surface. Conditions must be such, that the subject will not endanger themself. Individuals who have a painful neck, back or leg ailments or other injuries, should not attempt this test.

PROCEDURES FOR THE FINGER COUNT TEST

Step One

Instruction Stage and Demonstration

Explain, in the following manner, the instructions to be followed by the subject:

- **Tell the subject to stand or sit comfortably.**
- **Using either hand, count out loud while touching the tip of each finger with the tip of the finger. You must count exactly like this.** (Demonstrate how the thumb is used to count on the tip of each finger and further, how the subject must count out loud.
- **(1-2-3-4—4-3-2-1)**
- **Do this series three times.**
- **Do you understand?** (Make sure the subject indicates that he or she understands; if not, repeat the instructions and note the impaired cognitive thought processes).
- **Begin.**

Step Two

Performance

- **Observe the subject carefully to determine whether he or she performs the test as instructed and demonstrated.**

Step Three

Scoring Finger Count Test

- **Required additional instruction during testing.**
- **Used a hand other than the one designated.**
- **Missed touching all the proper fingers.**
- **Counted incorrectly.**
- **Was unable to accomplish the test.**

There are very few requirements for the Finger Count test. It can be used in place of the Modified Rhomberg Test or One-Leg Stand Tests when the subject complains of physical injuries or illnesses. An individual who has difficulty moving their fingers or is missing fingers should not attempt this test.

Important Notes About Field Sobriety Testing

No field sobriety tests should be conducted without the aid of an assisting officer. Remember the concept of Cover-Contact. Common sense dictates that when police officers are dealing with individuals who are intoxicated, extreme care should be taken to avoid injury to officers or to the subject. The purpose of the assisting officer is to provide protection for the investigator while he or she demonstrates and then evaluates the different Field Sobriety Tests.

The assisting officer should stand at a 45^0 angle to the rear of and within four feet of the subject. In this manner, the assisting officer can be ready to catch the subject if they fall or restrain the subject if he or she becomes violent. Moreover, there is no better witness

Standardized Symptomology

to the subject's FST performance than another well-trained police officer.

The following are symptoms associated with various drug types, which can be observed by conducting the Standardized Tests. They should be carefully noted and cataloged by the investigating officer.

Alcohol Intoxication

Horizontal Gaze Nystagmus	Observable
Vertical Gaze Nystagmus	Observable at High BAC levels
Rhomberg Stand	Slowed Internal Clock
Pupillary Size	Normal
Pupillary Reflex	Slowed

Central Nervous System Depressants

Horizontal Gaze Nystagmus	Observable
Vertical Gaze Nystagmus	Observable
Rhomberg Stand	Slowed Internal Clock
Pupillary Size	Normal
Pupillary Reflex	Slowed

Central Nervous System Stimulants

Horizontal Gaze Nystagmus	Not Observable
Vertical Gaze Nystagmus	Not Observable
Rhomberg Stand	Rapid Internal Clock
Pupillary Size	Dilated
Pupillary Reflex	Slowed

Cannabis

Horizontal Gaze Nystagmus	Not Observable
Vertical Gaze Nystagmus	Not Observable
Rhomberg Stand	Distorted Internal Clock
Pupillary Size	Normal or Slightly Dilated
Pupillary Reflex	Normal

Opiates

Horizontal Gaze Nystagmus	Not Observable
Vertical Gaze Nystagmus	Not Observable
Rhomberg Stand	Slowed Internal Clock
Pupillary Size	Constricted
Pupillary Reflex	Normal or Little Change

PCP

Horizontal Gaze Nystagmus	Observable
Vertical Gaze Nystagmus	Observable
Rhomberg Stand	Distorted Internal Clock
Pupillary Size	Normal
Pupillary Reflex	Normal

Inhalants

Horizontal Gaze Nystagmus	Observable
Vertical Gaze Nystagmus	Observable at High BAC Levels
Rhomberg Stand	Slowed Internal Clock
Pupillary Size	Normal or Bloodshot
Pupillary Reflex	Normal

Hallucinogens

Horizontal Gaze Nystagmus	Not Observable
Vertical Gaze Nystagmus	Not Observable
Rhomberg Stand	Distorted Internal Clock
Pupillary Size	Usually Dilated
Pupillary Reflex	Normal

SECTION FIVE: Evidence and Report Writing

EVIDENCE

The definition of evidence is:

"Articles and material which are found in connection with an investigation, and which aid in establishing the identity of the perpetrator, or the circumstances under which the crime was committed or which, in general, assists in the discovery of the facts."

In order to realize the full value of physical evidence, it must be cared for with an eye towards the sciences, as well as the law. A violation of statutory rules and agency policy and procedures, preservation/protection may lead to a full or partial loss of the value of the evidence and, in many circumstances, the loss of a case completely.

Evidence is divided into one or more of the following categories.

- **Corpus Delecti Evidence**
- **Associative Evidence**
- **Trace Evidence**

Corpus Delecti Evidence

Objects or substances, which are an essential part of the body of the crime. Examples of Corpus Delecti evidence are such items as Alcohol and Alcohol Containers, Narcotics and Drug Paraphernalia, Vehicles, Boats, Blood Samples, Alcohol Measurement Device Records, Video and Audio Recordings, etc.

Associative Evidence Evidence which links the suspect to the crime scene or offense. For example, a piece of broken taillight lenses from the scene of a hit and run collision.

Trace Evidence Objects or documents which assist the investigator in locating a suspect.

Procedure

An investigation may involve one or more of the mentioned types of evidence and evidence can be found in one or more of the categories. Before an object can become evidence, however, it must be recognized, by the DUI investigator, as being connected to the offense in some manner. On-the-job experience will assist in developing this skill, but education can broaden the officer's informational background.

The following skills will facilitate the development of the professional DUI Investigator:

- Knowledge of the laws of evidence and their applications to court procedure.
- Ability to recreate the events proceeding, during and after the commission of a crime.
- An ability to recognize indications of a modus operandi.
- Knowledge of the substantive law relating to the offense.
- Knowledge of scientific laboratory techniques and conclusions, which may be derived from their use.

The ability to recognize and gather valuable physical evidence must be supplanted by a knowledge of the correct procedure in caring for evidence from the time of its initial discovery until it is used or disposed of by a court. There are three important factors which must be considered before evidence will be allowed in a court of law:

- The object or document must be properly identified.
- Continuity or chain of custody must be established
- Competency must be proved – relevant and material.

Proof of Identity

The proof of identity implies that the investigator who first discovered the evidence can testify to its authenticity when it is admitted by a court. Quite simply, the investigator must be able to categorically state that no other piece of evidence has been substituted for the original object.

Proof of identity can be established by a systematic procedure that would ordinarily consist of the following steps:

1. Protection
2. Collection
3. Identification
4. Preservation
5. Transmission
6. Disposition

Chain of Custody

The number of persons who handle evidence, from the time of the commission of the alleged offense and the ultimate disposition in court, should be kept to a minimum. As an example, if a sample of blood is withdrawn, to determine the presence of Alcohol or Drugs, the chain of Custody, as a minimum, should be as follows:

1. Person collecting the sample.
2. Toxicology laboratory technician.
3. Back to the original officer collecting the sample.
4. Finally, given to the custody of the prosecutor.

Protection

The sample of evidence must be kept safe and secure from cross-contamination, and each transfer within the chain must be receipted. It is the responsibility of each transferee to insure that the evidence is accounted for during the time that it is in his/her custody.

> **NOTE: With regards to collecting a blood sample, make certain that the person doing so utilizes nonalcoholic antiseptic swabs. The investigator can then safely testify that the withdrawal site was not contaminated by any foreign substance. The individual who collected the sample may have to**

The protection of evidence serves two purposes:
1. Protection of fragile and/or perishable evidence.
2. Keeps the evidence, as near as possible, in the same condition as when it was originally collected.

Standards of Comparison

Known specimens to be utilized in court, as standards of comparison with the questioned evidence, are sometimes needed in establishing a subject's relationship to the offense under investigation. For example, Room Air versus Deep Lung Alveolar Air.

Containers and Packaging

Articles which can be removed and conveniently packaged should be placed in clean containers such as, envelopes, pillboxes, cardboard boxes, paper bags, etc. The choice of container will depend upon the size of the specimen, its fragility, physical state, whether solid or liquid, and whether it is to be transported by mail or hand delivered.

Storage and Preservation

Adequate facilities for storage of evidence should be maintained by the investigating agency, and equipped so that physical protection is assured against alteration or destruction from natural causes or unauthorized contacts.

Evidence in the form of organic matter, such as food, blood or tissue, may present special problems relating to preservation. In taking steps to prevent or delay deterioration, factors such as time and temperature must be taken into consideration. In warm weather, there should be a minimum of delay in placing the evidence in appropriate storage. Temperatures at or above 95^0 F greatly accelerate the decomposition of matter. At the same time, extreme cold may be detrimental to some specimens; blood, for example. The ideal temperature for blood or other perishable items is between 40^0 and 50^0 F.

NOTE: When dealing with evidence, it is important for the investigator to know and adhere to the policies and procedures of their specific agency.

REPORT WRITING

The effectiveness of a professional investigator is gauged, in large measure, by the reports that he or she submits with regards to a DUI arrest. If an otherwise superb investigation is poorly documented and reported, the reputation of the investigator suffers, and the case in question may be in jeopardy. This is due to the fact that numerous individuals will read the finished product, and pass judgment on the officer from what is written, or, perhaps more importantly, what is not written in the report.

The initial report establishes the basis of fact leading up to arrest of an individual, and it establishes the general nature and magnitude of the entire case. It is an objective summary of the facts and, as such, an invaluable tool to the arresting and assisting officers at a later date.

The writer of a DUI report should strive towards the basic qualities of the expository writing style: clarity and brevity, and the age-old tenants of the Police Report: completeness and accuracy. The questions of Who, What, When, Where, Why and How, must be answered. Specificity, however, is key to this type of writing style. It is not enough, to say that a vehicle swerved. The reporting officer must detail how this vehicle action occurred. If, during the trial, the defense attorney suddenly asks, "exactly where did the vehicle begin to swerve and what was the speed of my client's vehicle at the time?" The officer must know and be able to accurately answer the question. He or she cannot possibly recall all the details of the case 4 to 6 months after the arrest. The logical place for these answers is in the DUI report.

The report must annotate, in a logical progression, each event leading up to the arrest of the subject. Example: Driving Pattern, Observation of the Physical Demeanor of the subject, Field Sobriety Testing, Collection of the breath, blood and/or urine sample, etc.

Appending the initial report with witness statements, follow up reports of assisting officers, diagram, accident report, inventories, evidence card/s, etc, are critical for thoroughness and completeness.

It should be emphasized that police officers must report the facts in an objective manner. Facts that may lessen the impact of an individual's behavior must also be included. For example, note in the report if an individual had the smell of an alcoholic beverage on his/her breath, but did not show any significant outward manifestations of intoxication. The inclusion of this information will show that the investigator is above reproach and fair-minded.

Clear and simple language should be used in the arrest report. Confusing adjectives or police jargon must be avoided at all cost. In the case of a DUI arrest report, common situations will continuously present themselves and care should be taken to avoid stereotyping words or phrases. Politeness toward the subject is of paramount importance.

In many law enforcement jurisdictions, specialized report forms are used. Citation packets, alcoholic influence reports, preprinted initial reports and inventory lists, are but a few that can be found. Most are designed to promote efficient use of time but are in effect, only adequate in fulfilling the need for information. Professionalism demands that more data be obtained than is required by these forms. Make certain that all of the necessary information is included, using whatever time and materials necessary to complete the task.

In summary, law enforcement officers who strive toward excellence and professionalism in their report writing will find that their reputation in the offices of prosecuting and defense attorneys and courts of law are of the highest caliber, and that they cannot be impugned. Statistics prove that police officers that write concise, specific and accurate reports spend less time in court.

See pages 190, 191, 192 and 193 for an example of a DUI report. As stated before, careful scrutiny of the agency policies must be accomplished to be sure that the proper report is filed in police matter.

Report Narrative:

At approximately 02:30 hrs, 1/1/04, the above listed suspect vehicle was observed traveling northbound on Maple St., in a manner which suggested the possibility that the driver was impaired. The vehicle weaved significantly from one side of the roadway to the other. Specifically, it drifted from the northbound lane into the southbound lane and back multiple times. Twice, this vehicle motion encroached on the travel path of an oncoming southbound vehicle. The speed of the vehicle at the time of observation was generally 10 mph, while the prima facie limit at this location of Maple St. was 25 mph.

A traffic stop was effected at 1234 Maple St. When the police vehicle emergency lights were activated, the suspect vehicle moved slowly the to right hand curb and stopped without incident. The driver, identified by driver's license as the arrested person, was contacted and several Pre-Exit Tests were conducted.

A driver's license and registration were requested. The driver produced only the registration for the vehicle. The request for a driver's license was repeated. When the driver began to search for his license, he was asked where he was traveling from. He immediately stopped looking for the license and stated that he was on his way home. OBSERVATION: The driver's ability to divide his attention was impaired. He produced only one document when asked for two. He stopped looking for the drivers license when his attention was again divided. His response to the question was where he was going (home) and not where he had been. During this conversation, it was noticed that there was a moderate smell of alcoholic beverage coming from the interior of the vehicle. Further, when the driver turned his head and looked toward the outside of the vehicle, a moderate smell of alcoholic beverage came from his breath.

After a third request for a drivers license, he produced one. It identified the driver as Citizen, Joseph, DOB: 1/7/51.

At this point, Mr. Citizen was asked to exit the vehicle. When he got out of the driver's seat, he leaned on both the door and the left roof area of the suspect vehicle. Further, he leaned on the side of the vehicle as he walked to the rear where he had been directed to walk. OBSERVATION: Walking appeared to be difficult, in that he walked very stiff-legged and pigeon-toed. During this period of time, Mr. Citizen repeatedly asked why he was stopped. Although he was advised numerous times that he had been stopped due to a driving pattern which suggested the possibility of impaired driving, he could not or would not understand. OBSERVATION: Mr. Citizens' gross motor skills and cognitive thought processes were in fact impaired.

Given the driving pattern, the pre-exit tests and observed physical demeanor characteristics, Mr. Citizen was asked to take part in several field sobriety tests. He agreed to the tests, and the following were first demonstrated by this Reporting Officer and then undertaken by Mr. Citizen.

Prior to each test taking place, he was asked if he understood all of the instructions for each test, and he replied in the affirmative.

1) Horizontal Gaze Nystagmus –
   a) Jerking pursuit observed in both eyes.
   b) Nystagmus observed in both eyes at maximum deviation.
   c) Nystagmus observed in both eyes prior to 45^0.
   TOTAL SCORE: 6

2) Walk and Turn –
   a) The subject failed to remain in the instruction position until told to commence the Walking Stage
   b) He stepped off the line twice on the 5th and 6th steps away from the starting point
   c) Subject lost balance on the turn and nearly fell over
   d) Subject failed to keep his arms to his sides
   e) Subject was unable to complete the test as instructed
   TOTAL SCORE: 4

At this point, Mr. Citizen was arrested for Driving Under the Influence, based on the observed driving pattern, the observed physical demeanor, and the results of the field sobriety tests. He was searched, handcuffed, and secured in a police vehicle. He was then advised of the request that he take a test: specifically a breath test. Mr. Citizen refused at first, but changed his mind after being advised of the Implied Consent Law. He was then transported to the City Police Station, where the breath test was conducted. The result of the test was .113% BAC.

Investigative Process 193

Evidence in the form of the breath-testing device record and checklist, and a copy of the videotape showing activities at the scene of the traffic stop were secured in the evidence lockers. No evidence was located within the suspect vehicle, or on the person of Mr. Citizen.

SECTION SIX: Court Testimony

In every instance, in a court of law, the police officer is a witness. He or she is not an advocate for or against the defendant, and it is important that the Trier of Fact does not view an officer's testimony as biased or prejudicial against the defendant.

The jury is made up of people who, in large part, have only limited exposure to the criminal justice system by watching television or going to the movies. In fact, they are individuals who have lived in a vacuum as far as the criminal justice system is concerned. They are housewives, teachers, bankers, laborer, etc. They may be expert in their chosen fields of endeavor, but in general, do not have the slightest idea of what takes place in the system; yet, they may be the Trier of Fact.

On the other hand, in all probability, members of a jury have received a citation from a police officer, or have been a victim of crime and have had what they view as a bad experience. In effect, when police officers enter a courtroom, they face the most severe test of their professionalism and will face an uphill battle to gain the trust and confidence of the jury.

Pretrial Preparation

Before entering a court of law, all police reports should be reviewed thoroughly. Be prepared to answer any question that could conceivably be asked. Police reports may be utilized by the officer while testifying, but do not completely rely on them. Unless necessary, do not read from them verbatim while on the stand. The officers involved with the case should be sufficiently familiar with the contents of all the reports that they should be used only to refresh their memory. Also, because the investigation of a DUI offense is a team effort, review the reports of all the other officers involved in the situation.

Make certain that all evidence is available. If there were containers of alcoholic beverages, breath test device record, toxicology reports, and/or vials of the blood sample taken as evidence, be prepared to exhibit them in court and testify to their chain of custody.

Discussion of the case with the Prosecutor before the trial is something that every rookie learns in his or her police academy classes; nevertheless, it is something that must be emphasized. The United States Supreme Court has stated that "prosecutors are fungible" (a legal term meaning that prosecutors can be replaced at any time). It is common practice among prosecuting agencies to hand off files, and just as common for prosecutors to look at the file as they walk into court to select a jury. Do not walk into court with him or her without discussing the matter. Keep in mind that the defense attorney has had the case for a long period. They know every aspect of the case, including the history of the matter, and all the motions and actions dealt with during their dilatory tactics. Make certain to discuss any weaknesses or problems with regards to the case with the prosecutor. Make sure that they are prepared for them. It is better for the prosecution to bring the weaknesses out on direct examination. Again, fairness and openness will play in the prosecution's favor much more than the defense.

When a police officer is called into the courtroom to testify, he or she becomes the focus of attention for the members of the jury. **FIRST IMPRESSIONS DO MAKE A DIFFERENCE!** Uniformed officers should wear their uniforms or suit or sport coat/slack combination. The clothing should be clean and well-pressed giving a neat overall appearance. Officers from plain-clothes divisions should wear the appropriate attire for courtroom appearances. In most jurisdictions, this will be a suit or sport coat. Some courts may require that an officer, if they are wearing a uniform, lock up their weapons.

- Be careful of personal demeanor when not actively involved with the courtroom; i.e., hallway, cafeteria etc. The jury must perceive the officer as a professional; kind, courteous, and sensitive, off the stand as well as on. Never say anything in the courtroom that you would not want the jury to hear. Jurors who see an officer laughing and joking may feel their deportment is inappropriate for the situation.

- Be careful of conversing with defense attorneys. They are usually attempting to gather information that they can use later. Even something as innocuous as, "I've arrested this guy twice before," can be turned around and used against the officer in the courtroom. For example; "Officer, how many times have you had contact with my client?" "Isn't it true that you have arrested my client twice before?" The inference here is that you may not be as unbiased as a police officer should be, and may in fact be prejudiced toward the client. If you are on friendly terms with the defense attorney, keep the conversation on such topics as the weather or skiing conditions. Do no discuss the client without the prosecutor being present.

Testimony

Juries are instructed to pay attention to the demeanor of the witnesses as they are testifying. They will focus on the speech and the conduct of the officer as he or she enters the room; how they sit on the stand; and above all, the manner in which they answer questions put to them by the prosecution and the defense. While sitting on the witness stand, the officer should assume a relaxed position, without slouching. The hands should be neatly folded on their lap, or on the table in front of the stand.

Do not, under any circumstances, be argumentative, hostile, flippant or biased. The defense will capitalize on this attitude. Secondarily, if the officer is using energy to be angry, he or she will not be able to think clearly.

Maintain good eye contact with the attorneys and the jury. After taking the witness stand, glance shortly over the jurors, then turn attention to the prosecutor. Direct answers to the jury. The idea here is not to be condescending, but to make sure that the jury understands the concept of the offense being discussed.

At any rate, answer all questions specifically and directly. Speak loudly and clearly so that the jury and the court can hear. Avoid the use of police jargon, and speak in plain English. Example: "I got out of my car" instead of "I exited my vehicle." In other words, speak in conversational tones, as if narrating a story. Never refer to the defendant by the term "arrestee." Use courtesy titles, such as Mr., Mrs., Doctor, etc. Be candid with the answers given. If the answer is unknown to the officer, he or she should admit it. This type of testimony does not harm the officer or the case; indeed, it will increase their credibility with the jury. If either the prosecutor or the defense attorney asks a question that the officer is unable to answer, advise the judge that the question cannot be answered in the manner expressed. Provide truthful information. The judge will direct the attorney to rephrase the question.

Listen to each question carefully, and answer the questions that are asked. Do not second-guess. Do not give an answer based on what was thought to be asked. If the question is not understood, ask that it be repeated. Do not volunteer any information. Answer the question with a yes or no answer, whenever possible, and do not attempt to invent an answer. When a question is asked by either attorney, pause before answering. This gives an opportunity for an objection to be raised, and do not attempt to answer a question if an objection is raised. Wait until the judge and attorneys have settled the matter, and then answer if allowed by the judge.

If an officer forgets an answer, but it is known to be in a report, explain the lapse of memory to the court, then refer briefly to the report before answering. Again, do not read verbatim from the report.

Expert Testimony

A person is qualified to testify as an expert if he or she has special knowledge, skill, experience, training or education sufficient to qualify them as an expert on the subject to which the testimony relates.

Ordinarily, a witness must testify only to the known facts. They may not express an opinion or conclusion. (The exception to this opinion testimony is to the state of intoxication.) On the other hand, an expert witness deals almost exclusively in opinion testimony. Before he or she is allowed to express such an opinion however, it must be established to the court's (judges) standards, that he or she is indeed an expert – "they must be qualified." Questions with regards to training, experience and years as a police officer will be asked. With regards to the subject matter of this manual, an officer will be asked questions about:

- His or her training in DUI investigation.
- The number of times that he/she have dealt with an intoxicated person.
- How many investigations of intoxicated drivers he/she has undertaken.

More simply, expert testimony is a valuable means of arriving at the truth. It consists most commonly of experiments conducted to prove or disprove a fact or statement of the defendant, or one of the other witnesses.

Although a police officer must view him or herself as an objective collector of facts, and then an unbiased witness, others in the courtroom will look upon themselves as interested parties, ready to accuse a person of a crime on the slightest suspicion, or out of a particular zeal for prosecution. It is crucial, therefore, that the officer plays the part of an impartial and conscientious public servant endeavoring in a modest way to achieve the aims of justice. A calm and forthright presentation will convince the Trier of Fact of the honesty and integrity of the involved investigator.

This can be accomplished by following a few simple rules, which apply to both civilian and police witnesses:

1. Relate to the Court only what they know to be true.
2. Must have the appearance of candor, be courteous and responsive to answers.
3. Stay in control of emotions, and have the appearance and demeanor of a professional.

SECTION SEVEN: CASE LAW

UNIFORM VEHICLE CODE

The basis for our modern day DUI laws is a set of widely varied and often complex series of statues, ordinances and court precedent from almost every jurisdiction within the United States. Suffice it to say, that the operation of a vehicle by an intoxicated person has been a traffic offense from the earliest of time in the history of the automobile.

A standard set by the United States Government, known as the Uniform Vehicle Code, lists the following elements for the DUI offense:

1. A person under the influence of alcohol
2. Driving or being in actual control of a vehicle

The Supreme Court of Michigan

"It is gross and culpable negligence for a drinking man to drive and operate an automobile upon a public highway, and one doing and occasioning injuries to another, causing death, is guilty of manslaughter. It is unlawful for a defendant to operate his automobile upon the public highway while he is intoxicated; made unlawful be statute and wrong in and of itself...."

The Supreme Court of Vermont

"The primary object of this particular provision of this statutes on which the prosecution is based is the protection of the public from injury to person or property by persons operating or attempting to operate motor vehicles while under the influence of intoxicating liquor or drugs on our highways, and if it can fairly

be done, the statutes must be construed as to accomplish the purpose for which they were intended. . . . "

The Supreme Court of Vermont

"It is a truism that a person who is even to the slightest extent 'under the influence of liquor,' in the common and well understood acceptation of the term, is to some degree at least less able, either mentally or physically, or both, to exercise the clear judgment and steady hand necessary to handle as powerful and dangerous mechanism as a modern automobile, with safety to himself and the public. With the increasing number and speed of automobiles on our highways, and the appalling number of accidents resulting therefrom, it is not strange that the law making power determine that any person who of his own free will, voluntarily lessened in the slightest degree his ability to handle such vehicles by the use of intoxication liquor should, while in such condition, be debarred from their true use. The legislature has placed no limitations on the extent of the influence required, nor can we add to their language nor will it follow, as appellant seems to fear, that every man who has taken a drink falls within the ban of this statute. If that drink does not cause him to be 'influenced' in the ordinary and well understood meaning of the term, he is not affected by the law. If he is so influenced, he must bear the consequences of his voluntary act by refraining from driving an automobile the influence lasts. . . ."

The Ohio Court of Appeals

"In our opinion, being under the influence of alcohol or intoxicating liquor means that the accused must have consumed some intoxicating beverage, whether mild or potent, and in such a quantity, whether small or great, that the effort thereof on him was to adversely affect his actions, reaction, conduct, movement or mental processes or to impair his reactions, under the circumstance then existing so as to deprive him of that clearness of intellect and control of himself which he would otherwise possess. It is not necessary to find the accused in a high state of excitement, enthusiasm, elation, frenzy or delirium, or even pugnacious to find him under the influence, as it is common knowledge that some persons react to the influence of liquor by becoming dull, sleepy, dejected or sad. And it is common knowledge also that different people react differently at different times. Physical condition, mental strain, lack of food, and temperamental variation in individuals affect in varying degrees the tolerance of the same individuals to alcohol as these conditions increase or decrease with such individuals from time to time. So, it is important that the effect on his actions and reactions under the circumstances then existing be borne in mind. It is not how many drinks of this or that the accused had. A drink is not the same to all persons. There is a difference between a sip and three finger, yet each may be some persons drink. It is not a question of how much liquor would have such and such an effect upon an ordinary person. The question is what effect did the liquor the accused consumed have on him at the time under consideration...."

It is obvious from the above interpretations, that there is a distinct difference between the term "intoxicated person" and "intoxicated driver." This is due to the complex nature of the task of driving a motor vehicle.

The level or standard of intoxication for the driver of a vehicle is much lower than that of a person or pedestrian. It must be emphasized that although the courts have established a lower standard for the driver of a motor vehicle, they have reserved the authority to interpret what is defined as intoxication on a case-by-case basis.

The Trier of Fact will base decisions on the testimony of all persons involved.

The Supreme Court of Indiana
"It is not necessary for a driver to be drunk in order to violate the statue making it unlawful for a person to operate a motor vehicle upon a public highway while under the influence of intoxicating liquor; nor is it necessary to prove any specific degree of intoxication, but in each case where a person is charged with a violation of the provisions of the act, the question as to whether the defendant was under the influence of intoxicating liquor is one of fact to be determined by the court or jury from all the circumstances of the case...."

In the past, a great deal of controversy arose over the use of the term "under the influence" affecting the mental or physical faculties.

It was thought that even though a person was under the influence affecting his or her physical faculties, but not his or her mental faculties, he/she was not in violation of the offense. Therefore, investigators had to prove that both mental and physical faculties were affected.

This is not the case in our modern times.

The Superior Court of New Jersey

We cannot accept the theory advanced by the defendant that the court in State v. Rogers, supra, laid down the rule that when one so charged, as here, has his mental faculties unimpaired, yet is lacking in physical control or coordination of his body brought about by drinking of intoxicating liquor, he may still with impunity operate his automobile on the highways of this State. We think the words 'which tend to deprive him of that clearness of intellect and control of himself which he would otherwise possess' are not restricted in their meaning to a lack of coordination of the body, and, in addition thereto, an impairment of mental faculties, but rather to a lack of control brought about by the drinking of intoxicating liquor to the extent that he cannot control himself due to an impairment of either his mental faculties or physical capabilities."

The courts of our land have struggled over the term "driving," as it applies to a DUI offense.

In early histories of the statutes, driving meant that the vehicle had to be in "motion" for there to be a violation of the offense. During the evolution of the law, however, the strict definition of driving was diluted to indicate that "motion" was not a strict requirement for a person to have been actually driving the vehicle.

Certainly, movement of a vehicle is an essential element of the offense, defined by DUI statutes', nevertheless, motion does not always constitute "driving."

The West Virginia Supreme Court
"To 'drive' a vehicle necessarily implies a driver or operator and affirmative or a positive action on the part of the driver. A mere movement of the vehicle might occur without any affirmative act by the driver, or, in fact by any person. If a vehicle is moved by some power beyond the control of the driver, or by accident, is not such an affirmative or positive action on the part of the driver as will constitute a driving of the vehicle within the meaning of the statute."

As time went by and the courts began to indicate the need for a more descriptive term, the courts held that no movement was needed to constitute an offense under the statutes. It was enough that a subject manipulated the mechanical or electrical functions of the vehicle; nevertheless, the driver had to maintain or have the ability to manipulate the controls of the motor vehicle.

However, once again the Uniform Vehicle Code issued its interpretations, expanding on the term "operate," and again made a substitution with the term "actual physical control." Over a period of time, the states began to incorporate this term into their statutes.

"Actual physical control" indicates that a driver had "present physical ability and/or influence over a vehicle."

The Supreme Court of Montana

"Using the term in 'actual physical control' in its composite sense, it means 'existing' or 'present bodily restraint' directing influence, domination or regulation.' Thus, if a person has existing or present bodily restraint, directing influence, domination or regulation, of an automobile, while under the influence of intoxicating liquor, he commits a misdemeanor within the provisions of the statute."

"The above definition makes it apparent that movement of the vehicle isn't necessary to charge an offense under this provision of the statute. Thus, one could have 'actual physical control' while merely parking or standing still so long as one was keeping the car in restraint or in position to regulate its movement. Preventing a car from moving is as much control and dominion as actually putting the car in motion on the highway. Could one exercise any more regulation over a thing, while bodily present, than prevention of movement or curbing movement? As long as one were physically or bodily able to assert dominion, in the sense of movement, then he has as much control over an object as if he were actually driving the vehicle."

The definition of the "vehicle" or "motor vehicle" used in the offense of DUI has been debated over and over again, ad nauseam, in courts of the land. Irregardless of which term is used, the definition, as put forth by the Uniform Vehicle Code, is used extensively by the Appellant Courts; that is "Self Propelled," or "was designated for self-propulsion."

The Supreme Court of Vermont

"Manifestly, it was design, mechanism and construction of the vehicle, and not its temporary condition, that the Legislature had in mind when framing the definition of a motor vehicle. Neither the authorities nor sound logic admit of a different conclusion."

Various State statutes have indicated that an offense can be committed anywhere, and not just on the "public highway."

This has obviously caused some consternation to the defendant convicted of DUI while in their own driveways.

The Supreme Court of Iowa

"Automobiles have been declared dangerous instrumentalities, and it can be readily understood why their operation by intoxicated persons would not be allowed anywhere, for the very good reason that the influence of liquor upon the human mind is such that the addict might not remain off the public way, but because of said very loss of self control, wander or recklessly drive the machine in front of or over others legitimately using the road, often times causing injury, destruction or death."

The Supreme Judicial Court of Maine

"It is apparent that the Legislature appreciated that the menace was the same to people using private ways, driveways and any

other places where motor vehicles might be operated. These people should be protected against the intoxicated driver of a motor vehicle. They should not lose the benefit of that protection the instant they step from the line of a public way into a private way or driveway. The Legislature evidently intended to safeguard the rights of all persons who might be endangered without limitation to those on public ways or even confining the protection to places where the public had the right of access. The very purpose of operating a motor vehicle is to go somewhere. Even assuming that a man, realizing his condition, decided to drive his car into his own garage, yet the law, as we construe it, intended to protect his child or any other person who might be upon the driveway, even to the stranger within his gates. We are not dealing with the rights of litigants on the civil side of the court, but with the criminal statute."

Various states have adopted, and the Uniform Vehicle Code has recommended, the adoption of "absolute laws." These are statutes that specifically state an amount of ETOH; that is, Per Se intoxication. As can be imagined, there have been court challenges to the constitutionality of these types of laws.

The Delaware High Court
"The statute provides for no presumption of guilt, but instead provides that any person having the specified alcohol concentration 'shall be guilty'. To establish guilt, the State must prove only that the defendant was in physical control of the

vehicle, and that a proper and timely test showed the required percentage of alcohol concentrated in the defendants system."

The courts have held that there is indeed a connection between the presumption of a person being "under the influence," and specific alcohol concentrations in the blood.

The Arizona Supreme Court
"Medical science has established the fact that there is a rational and logical relationship between the percentage by weight of alcohol contained in the blood flowing through a persons body and that persons state or condition of being 'under the influence' of alcohol. Sobriety of an individual decreases as the percentage of alcohol in his blood increases."

"Ordinarily, only those facts or elements of a crime constitute an offense. However, when dealing with DUI, it is important to understand that, although there may not be a mention of erratic or reckless driving, they are an inherent part of the matter and it is not necessary to show recklessness or erratic driving to have a violation of the statute. If an individual is operating any vehicle on any highway while under the influence of alcohol, the person is doing so in violation of the law. It is not necessary to show that damage resulted from the operators condition or that he drove in a bizarre or erratic manner."

The Supreme Court of Massachusetts

"It is wholly immaterial whether the defendant exercised due care to avoid injury to other travelers, and he could be convicted even if there were no travelers on the street."

The Texas Court of Appeals

"The law does not withhold its forbiddance until an intoxicated man on the highway kills somebody or wrecks his own or some other car. If he is drunk, or is under the influence of intoxicants, he is forbidden to drive an automobile on a public highway in this State, and the law is violated when he does so drive his car, as much if he keeps to the middle of the road or if he wrecks a dozen cars."

Remember that reckless driving is the manner in which a vehicle is driven, and does not have anything to do with the impairment of the Central Nervous System. A perfectly sober person may drive in a reckless manner due to a desire to do so, and not out of impairment of the mental processes. It is simply a matter of protecting the public safety that persons may be punished for an offense such as DUI, even if nonrecklessness is shown.

This training manual has stressed the concept that not only alcohol, but that certain drugs and/or polycombinations, impair the CNS. This is truly a menace to the pedestrian and driving public.

The pervasiveness of drug consumption has increased at an incredible and alarming rate. Challenges to statutes which state "drugs" or the phrase "to a degree which renders them incapable of safely driving," as unduly vague, have been struck down, thus allowing their use in contemporary statutes.

The Supreme Court of Maine
"This court takes judicial notice of the well recognized fact that overindulgences or consumption of drugs and if he operates a motor vehicle while in that condition, is guilty of a violation of law."

In California, Officers stopped a vehicle which passed them at a 70 mph rate of speed. Officers also observed "weaving" within the travel lane and the driver was stopped and administered field sobriety tests.

The driver was found to be impaired, although officers did not detect an odor of alcoholic beverage about the person.

The California Superior Court
"She was stopped because of a speeding violation, attended by circumstances suggesting a lack of control over the vehicle. The phenomena exhibited by the defendant to Nezet (arresting officer) were those of an intoxicated person, and no doubt the most common cause in the experience of police was alcoholic intoxication. Nezet was competent to form an opinion as to whether defendant was intoxicated."

> *"Nezets opinion that defendant was under the influence of something reasonably envisaged the possibility defendant was under the influence of intoxicating liquor, a matter concerning which he was competent to testify, without experiential training. Defendant, however, had no odor of alcohol about her and Nezet thought questioning her as what she had been taking would have been improper after her mention of her attorneys. The probability that defendants condition was produced by alcohol having been tentatively eliminated, it became reasonable to entertain and hold a strong suspicion that defendant was under the influence of a narcotic."*

Even though it is not necessary to show erratic or reckless driving in "drug" cases, it is necessary to demonstrate that a person was impaired and, therefore, was "unable to safely operate a vehicle."

No one has been able to quantify the amount of any drug as intoxicating.

As DUI investigators, results must illustrate:
1. An impairing drug was consumed by the subject.
2. That the subject was impaired in the same sense as alcohol intoxication.

Two other California cases involving "under the influence of drugs" state the need for the description of impairment leading to arrest.

People v. Davis

"In the case at bench the defect is lack of proof that defendant had used narcotics, but the total lack of any evidence was impaired. There was neither expert opinion nor the observation anyone that defendant lacked the alertness, judgment and coordination which are needed to operate a motor vehicle in a prudent and cautious manner."

"As used in section 23102 'under the influence' means that the intoxicating had so far affected the nervous system, brain or muscles as to impair to an appreciable degree the ability to operate the vehicle in a manner like that of an ordinary prudent and cautious person in the full possession of his faculties, using reasonable care and under like circumstances. We see no reason why the forgoing definition should not apply also to the definition of the term 'under the influence' as used in section 23105 (drugs)."

Our society is one which is greatly dependent on the use of prescription drugs. It is common to hear from a driver, "BUT OFFICER, MY DOCTOR TOLD ME TO TAKE THEM. . . ."

The courts have long held that with regards to traffic law, knowledge of one's physical or mental condition is of paramount importance to preserve public safety.

It is incumbent on each driver to realize his/her respective conditions and refrain from driving if their condition is such that the safety of the public is endangered.

Harrell v. City of Norfolk
"The defense urged, that the pills were taken on the advice of the dentist and in ignorance of the ultimate result, is more specious than real. The instruction of the dentist to the defendant was to 'take one pill in the event his tooth hurt him and he could not sleep.' This should have been notice to the defendant that the pills, when taken, would produce drowsiness. Notwithstanding the fact that defendant had taken one pill earlier in the evening, he proceeded to drink two highballs during the progress of the party, and before starting for Norfolk proceeded to take two more pills, instead of one as advised by the dentist. Whether the influence of the whiskey or the influence of the drug predominated, there is no doubt that defendant condition, while driving his automobile, presented a menace to persons on the street at that early hour of the morning."

The opinion of witnesses, though not necessarily always admitted in criminal trials, can and have almost always been used in the trial of a DUI offender.

The courts have ruled that an ordinary layman can easily discern a state of intoxication and, therefore, can testify in a court of law as to their opinion. To prove that a person was intoxicated, it is not necessary to prove the process or how they became intoxicated.

The state of intoxication is a condition wherein even a lay witness may express his opinion.

The credibility of the witness is enhanced if, along with his or her opinion, they gave specific details as to the state of intoxication. It was testified that he was unsteady on his feet, his walk was unusual, he staggered along, his speech was thick, faulty, and not clear, and he had the odor of alcoholic beverage on his breath. This evidence was competent and sufficient to sustain a finding of the jury that he was at the time important to this case under the influence of intoxicating liquor.

The rule, as deduced from the weight of authority, is that a witness may testify, from observation, whether a person was intoxicated. "Intoxication is a fact which a witness may ascertain in the same manner in which he ascertains other facts. He may give the details and then may state the ultimate fact of intoxication as derived from observation."

It has been shown that in the case of intoxication, an expert witness holds no more authority than that of a layman. Both testimonies carry the same weight in a court of law, as the state of intoxication has universally known outward indications. This does not mean that the State is relieved of the burden of proving the other elements of the offense. It must still show that the subject was operating a vehicle, or was in actual physical control, and was in the State, etc.

As in all cases of criminal violations, evidence is of critical importance to show that indeed a crime was committed, and to show the manner in which the violation occurred. The evidence will take the form of either physical property and/or oral testimony.

"The videotaped evidence of an arrestee's slurred speech, in response to routine booking questions, and his performance of sobriety tests is non-testimonial, and not within the scope of the Fifth Amendment privilege against compelled self-incrimination."

"In the case, the defendant was arrested for driving while intoxicated, and while at the police station, was recorded by video tape, including his slurred speech in response to routine booking questions, and his performance of various sobriety tests. During the course of taking the sobriety tests, he made several unsolicited incriminating statements, but was not advised of his Miranda Rights until after the booking process, after which he answered the routine booking questions and took sobriety tests."
"That all of the defendant's videotaped words and actions at the police station were admissible at the trial, except his response concerning the date of his sixth birthday. The Court stated that while his inability to articulate words in a clear manner in response to routine booking questions was not testimonial, his response to the sixth birthday question was testimonial, because from the content of the response, it could be inferred that his mental state was confused.

The Court also found that his performance of the sobriety tests was non-testimonial and that the incriminating statements he made while performing the tests were not in response to interrogation."

INDEX

A

Absorption
  of drugs and alcohol, 39, 55
Ability
  to change, 6
Acetaldehyde, 79
Acetic Acid, 79
Acute Effect
  Mallenby Effect, 77
Adaptation, 22
Admissions, 130
Agency Policy, 182
Alcohol, 8
Alcohol Concentrations
  of 4% to 50%, 55
  within the human body, 59
  function of weight to volume, 59
Alcohol Dehydrogenase (ADH), 79
Alcoholic Beverage, 54
beer, 55
brandy, 55
bourbon, 55
whiskey, 55
wine, 55
Amyl, 50
Ancillary Structures, 7
Associators, 19, 22, 27

B

Basic Unit
  of behavior, 37
Beer, 55
Biased, 194, 197
Blood Alcohol Calculations, 60
  Widmarks Formula, 60
  ounces of pure alcohol, 61
  number of drinks, 62
Blood Alcohol Concentration (BAC), 63
Blood to Breath, 79
Brain, 7, 9, 27
  Cerebellum, 14
Cerebral Cortex, 11
  Cerebrum, 10
Forebrain, 10
Frontal Lobe, 12
Hindbrain, 14
Hypothalamus, 13
  Longitudinal Cerebral Fissure, 11
Medulla Oblongata, 15
Occipital Lobe, 12
  Parietal Lobe, 12
Pons, 15
  Reticular Formation, 13
  Substantia Nigra, 13
  Temporal Lobe, 12
  Thalamus, 13
Ventral Tegmental Area, 13
Brain Stem, 13
Bridge, 15 Uniform Vehicle Code, 201

C

Carbonated Beverages, 56
Case Law, 201
Arizona Supreme Court, 210
California Superior Court, 212
Delaware Supreme Court, 209
Harrell v. City of Norfolk, 215
Ohio Court of Appeals, 203
People v. Davis, 214
Superior Court of New Jersey, 205
Supreme Court of Indiana, 204
Supreme Court of Iowa, 208
Supreme Court of Massachusetts, 211

Supreme Court of Michigan, 201
   Supreme Court of Montana, 207
Supreme Court of Vermont, 201, 202, 208
   Supreme Judicial Court of Maine, 208, 212
Texas Court of Appeals, 211
Uniform Vehicle Code, 201
   West Virginia Supreme Court, 206
Cells, 4
Cellular Bodies, 4
Central Nervous System, 4, 36, 37
Cerebrospinal Function, 19
Club Drugs, 105
Cold Remedies, 54
Communicate Thoughts, 7, 133
Competency, 64
Complex Emotional Feelings, 6
Computer, 7
Conduct of the Officer, 197
Control of Inhibitions, 134
Court Testimony, 194
Creatin, 32
Creative Thoughts, 6, 11

D

Decision Making, 6
Defense Attorneys, 196
Depolarization, 24
Depressants, 83
Difficulty
   in exiting vehicle, 132
   in focusing, 134
   In following directions or instructions, 126
   in manipulating devices or documents, 132
   in performing tasks/fine motor skills, 127
in standing or walking
Diffusion, 80
Distallation, 52
Distribution, 57, 58
Divided Attention, 126, 127, 132
   important symptoms of, 132
   multiple requests, 128
   rapid follow up questions, 128
   unusual questions, 128
Documentation, 130
Driving
actual physical control, 113
competence, 8
operating, 112
patterns, 114 - 120
under The Influence, 38

Drug
   action, 46
   dose, 47
   time, 48
   route of administration, 48
definition, 42
misuse and abuse, 43
trends, 43
Drunk, 67

E

Effector, 19, 31
Elements of DUI Offense, 112
Elimination, 78
breathing process, 79
   Henry's Law, 80, 81
evaporation, 79
excretion, 79
   metabolism, 79
   perspiration, 79

Emotional Instability, 132
Ethyl Alcohol, 50, 51, 52
ETOH, 53
Euphoria, 68
Evidence, 182
   associative, 182
   definition of, 182
   trace
corpus delecti, 182
identification, 184
organic matter, 186
original object, 184
physical, 182, 183
preservation, 184
proof of identity, 184
protection, 184, 185
Expert, 194, 199
Extrapolation, 63
Exogenous Drugs, 8

F

Feelings, 6
Female
   55% water, 58
Fermentation, 51
Field Sobriety Tests, 113, 131, 135
   elements of, 141
   finger count, 177

horizontal gaze nystagmus, 138, 141, 142
    Daubert Standard, 152
Frye Standard, 149
overview, 141
    observable, 179, 180
    not observable, 179, 180, 181
    one leg stand, 138
    testing procedure, 156
    walk and turn, 162
    testing procedures, 162
    modified rhomberg, 174
    test procedures 174
one-leg stand, 169
    testing procedures, 169
research and development, 134
validation, 139
Folia, 14
Fungible, 195

G

Gender Differences, 58
Glands
    duct, 34
    endocrine, 35
Gross Motor Control, 132

H

Hallucinogens, 98
Henry's law, 81
Hostile, 197
Human Being
    or person, 112
Human Biological Potential, 3
Human Intellect, 3, 36
    and reasoning, 36

I

Impairment, 67
    balance and coordination, 132, 134
    central nervous system, 125
    cognitive thought processes, 132
Incoherence, 126
Intellect, 5, 7
Intoxication, 67
    eyes
        glazed, 134
        blurring, 73
loss of visual perception, 73

    non-focusing, 134
    vision, 132, 135
    high level, 132, 134
higher mental functions, 133
inability to comprehend, 126
low level, 133, 134
    lower mental functions 133
moderate, 132, 134
physical characteristics, 71
    cognitive thought, 72
hearing, 71
    malnutrition, 72
    muscular coordination, 72
smell, 71
    taste, 71
    vasodilation, 72
    vision, 73
low, 126
moderate, 126
severe, 126
unimpaired mental/physical abilities, 131
    urination or defecation in clothing, 126
    with regards to operating a vehicle, 67
Investigative Process, 111

J

Judgment, 11, 68
    social inhibitions, 68
    self evaluation, 68
    risk assessment, 69
    euphoria, 69
    perception of reality, 69

K

Kinesthetics, 15
Knowledge
    laws of evidence, 183

L

Lapse of Memory, 198
Legal Concepts, 112
Legal Sanctions, 111

M

Male
    70% water, 58

Mallenby Effect, 77
Medical Usage, 52
Memory, 6, 11
Metablism, 78
Methyl Alcohol Poinsoning, 54
Mood Swings, 134
Mumbling
   unintelligible speech, 126
Muscles
   cardiac, 33
   contractile, 31
     irritable, 32
     extensible, 32
     elastic, 32
   fine motor control, 33
   tone, 32
   skeletal, 33
   smooth, 33

N

Nerve
   afferent, 27
   cables, 27
     efferent,
        motor, 27
     ganglia, 27
   tracts, 27
Neuron, 22
Neurotransmitters, 25
Nystagmus
   aural, 154
   caloric, 153
   cheyne-stokes, 154
   disassociative, 154
   fixation, 154
   head, 155
   labyrintine, 155
   miners, 155
   occular, 155
   optokinetic. 154, 155
   oscillating, 155
   palatal, 155
   panoptic, 155
   pendular, 155
   physiologic, 154
   positional alcoholic, 154
   post-rotational, 153
   railroad, 155
   retraction or refractory, 155
   rhythmical, 155
   rotary, 155
   rotational, 153
   undulating, 155
   unilateral, 156
   vestibular, 155
   vibratory, 156
   visual, 156

O

Obesity
   less water per pound of body weight, 58
Opinion
   level of BAC, 64
Oxidize, 79

P

Performance
   specific task, 67
Peripheral Nervous System, 17
   somatic, 17
   autonomic, 18
   sympathetic, 18
   parasympathetic, 18
Person, 112
   physical demeanor, 113, 123, 125
     observe and document, 125
Personal Demeanor, 196
Phosphagen, 32
Phosphoric Acid, 32
Police Report, 194
Probable Cause, 112
   moving traffic violations, 123
   vehicle equipment violations, 123
Process Incoming Information, 133
Professional Police Officer, 63
Prosecutor, 195
Psycho-Physical Examination, 131
Pupillary Reflex
   normal, 181
Pupillary Size
   constricted, 180
   dilated, 179
   normal, 179, 180
   usually dilated, 181

R

Reason, 6, 11, 36
   need for, 38